Portugal

The Provinces from South to North

CONTENTS

Part 1
This is Portugal 3
Essential details in brief 5
The Portuguese way of life 6
Signposts of History 10
Phases of History 11
Two thousand years of Art 13
Food and Drink 16
Holidays in Portugal 18

Part 2
Hints for your holiday 22

Where to go and what to see 23
Lisbon 23
The Algarve landscape 34
From the Tagus to the Algarve 57
Portugal's little known North 61
The Island provinces in the Atlantic 89

Part 3
Useful things to know 92
Before you go 92
Getting to Portugal 93
During your stay 94

Useful words and phrases 96

Index Inside back cover

Maps and Plans
Lisbon (town plan) 27
Estremadura 33
Lagos district 38
Faro district 46
Estremoz district 58
Oporto (town plan) 64
Oporto district 67
Map of Portugal Back cover

Estoril

This is Portugal

Portugal, Britain's oldest ally, is quite often considered as just a geographical extension of Spain. This is far from true. Portugal is still comparatively unaffected by large-scale tourism and is one of the most rewarding holiday venues of western Europe. Woods, fields and meadows, vineyards, large orchards and acres of vegetables blend in with mountain ranges, valleys, plains, rocky coastlines and sandy beaches. One of the mountains, the Torre, rises to a height of 1,991 m, and although the river network is not as extensive as in Spain, the Tagus forms a large lake at Lisbon. More so even than Spain, Portugal is very much a maritime country, with no point more than 170 km from the Atlantic coast. The difference between Portugal and Spain is also noticeable in the people. The Portuguese are more sentimental, and more reserved, although as always there are exceptions. They are reliable, have high standards of cleanliness and are by tradition very friendly.

There is one other misunderstanding. Portugal does not just consist of Lisbon and the Algarve. If you are interested in touring or in educational trips, you will find Portugal a real gold mine, but you will need to allow yourself plenty of spare time there. There is an abundance of sleepy villages, ornate churches, cloistered cathedrals, magnificent châteaux and palaces, and museums both famous and less well known, all covering the various eras of the country's history. Many of these can be found with ease, while others will be discovered quite unexpectedly along the way. The seaside resorts on the west coast, the vineyards, and the farmlands of the Costa Verde have gained much in importance over the years.

Tourism

Many people think that Portugal is a place to go to only in the summer, but the early spring and autumn are both equally inviting, while Lisbon and its environs, as well as the Algarve, attract winter visitors, not only those interested in ethnology but also gourmets, golfers, anglers and walkers.

It is no longer correct to say that Portugal is more expensive than Spain. In fact prices are very much on a par when it comes to accommodation. All-in tours to Spain may well be cheaper, but this probably has more to do with flight distances and special offers from charter companies than with living costs. However, it is really not surprising that Portugal, despite its potential as a holiday destination, is still relatively little known. From the point of view of tourism, it did spend a long period as a 'Sleeping Beauty', as it were — with the exceptions of Lisbon, the health resorts of Estoril and Cascais, and Funchal on Madeira.

Since the sixties, though, foreign tourism has developed at a tremendous rate, especially in the Algarve, where modern holiday centres have sprung up as if overnight. Standards of service have unfortunately not always kept pace with the building boom. The stream of resettlement from the former Portuguese colonies brought with it additional problems and internal unrest. Many visitors at that time returned home with a feeling of dissatisfaction, which naturally did little to promote Portugal as a holiday country. Today, however, Portugal is a place where you can get good value for your money.

For those who know exactly what they want from a holiday, who seek out all relevant information about what they can expect to find in the resorts they are considering, and who then make their choice, Portugal will certainly not disappoint. This travel guide aims to provide the kind of information required in such situations. It should also help those who have already decided to visit Portugal not to miss any of its beautiful sights. Anyone who has not seen Portugal, be it only Lisbon or the rocky coastline of the Algarve, cannot say that he knows Europe.

Here, at its south-western end (or beginning), it is quite different from the way people imagine it — far more pleasant...

Essential details in brief

Name:	República Portuguesa (Republic of Portugal).
Founded:	October 5th 1910. Formerly known as the Kingdom of Portugal (since A.D. 1143). The current legal constitution dates from April 2nd 1976.
Form of Government:	Parliamentary Democracy.
Head of State:	President who is also the Commander-in-Chief of the armed forces. Elected by the people for a five-year term of office. Appointed head of the government as the result of a parliamentary election.
Representative body:	Parliament with 250 delegates. Four-year legislative period.
Parties:	Democratic Alliance (three-party alliance, made up of Social Democrats, Social Democratic Centre Party and the Pro-Monarchic People's Party), the Socialist Party, the Communist Party and several smaller parties.
Territory:	92,082 sq. km comprising 11 mainland provinces plus the Azores and Madeira. It is divided for administrative purposes into 22 Districts. In addition Macao (15.7 sq. km; pop. 280,000), in the Far East, is an independent territory under Portuguese administration.
Population:	10.3 million.
Growth rate:	1% approx.
Religion:	99% Roman Catholic with a small number of Protestants (about 40,000) and Jews (about 6,000).
Life expectancy:	69 years on average.
Important exports:	Textiles, machinery, chemical products, cork, resin, wine, canned fish, olive oil.
Vital imports:	Petroleum, grain, iron and steel, machinery, vehicles, foodstuffs.
Important trading partners:	Great Britain, West Germany, France, Italy, U.S.A., Spain, Japan and Angola.
Other information:	Portugal is a member of UNO, NATO, OECD and EEC.

The Portuguese way of life

It is not only the country but also the Portuguese people who differ from the way we think of them. Fiery southerners? Not in the least! Their way of thinking is almost English. They are extremely polite, reserved, calm, very keen on good manners and fair play, especially when it comes to bullfighting, the *Tourada*. In contrast to neighbouring Spain, it is the bull which has the advantage in Portugal and it is never killed. The Matador carries out only the traditional movements without actually lunging with his sword, while the Toreadors outsmart the bull, eventually forcing it to the ground. Nevertheless, the Portuguese have a lot in common with their Iberian neighbours. They are quite as proud as the Spanish, above all in their dealings with the Spaniard himself. The visitor who is proficient in languages will very quickly notice this if he tries to communicate in Spanish. Although understood, he is seldom answered, but anyone who tries to make himself understood by pointing, gesticulating or using only the slightest smattering of Portuguese will have no problem and the person addressed will do all he can to help.

'Amanhã' — tomorrow

The visitor to Portugal must, however, have plenty of time and patience. 'Tomorrow' is the operative word, as in Spain, but *amanhã* is the term used instead of *mañana*. Hardly anything gets done immediately, which does not matter very much to the Portuguese as it is all part of everyday life and is completely normal. Everyone seems to be quite resigned to this state of affairs, although sometimes it can prove to be annoying. It is an attitude described by the Portuguese as *saudade* and finds expression in the *fado*, a type of melancholy music played in a minor key, full of many different pitches and almost always accompanied by mournful words. The dictator Salazar felt that it had an adverse influence and consequently ordered it to be banned, which was quite unforgivable! All attempts to implement this instruction were stubbornly ignored.

This outlook on life can have a certain appeal to the tourist who must also accept that the Portuguese, tolerant as they are, can have strong views on many things. Anyone who attempts, for instance, to enter a church in a T-shirt, shorts or a bikini will be politely but firmly refused admittance. Appropriate dress is expected in first-class hotels and good restaurants as well as when going to a theatre or opera house, although for men this would not necessarily mean a suit and tie.

'Plus ça change'

In spite of revolution and sweeping change, Portugal has remained a conservative country. This is evident at cinemas, which seldom show sex films, and in the complete absence of prostitutes. Unless men have marriage in mind, Portuguese women tend to shun them, although, as usual, there are always exceptions. In the capital, Lisbon, and in the elegant seaside resorts of Estoril and Cascais, as well as in some of the holiday towns in the Algarve, attitudes to life are more relaxed. Contrasts in living standards are as pronounced as are the differences in life-style between the holiday centres and the rural areas. In some cases in the provinces, living conditions are almost medieval. The primitive houses are certainly very picturesque and photogenic but are almost always without sanitation and often without electricity or running water.

The Portuguese thoroughly enjoy social life. Bars, pubs and street cafés can never

The Portuguese way of life

Traditional dancing at an Algarve wedding

complain of lack of customers. The numerous festivals always attract the whole of the population — with music, dancing, floral decorations, *son et lumière* and fireworks. As can be seen, the Portuguese are a quite unusual people, difficult to put into ordinary categories. Anyone who is prepared to accept this, and adapt just a little, will certainly feel at home in this beautiful country.

How the Portuguese make a living

Agriculture
If one tries to think of typical Portuguese products, port wine and cork are practically the only ones that come to mind. These two well known exports, however, do not play a crucial role in the domestic economy of the Portugal of today. The country is indeed the largest exporter of cork in the world (more than half the total world production), yet textiles (20% of the export trade), machinery and chemicals play a much more important part in foreign trade. Portugal, however, is predominantly an agricultural country. Almost half of the country's total surface area is devoted to farming and over one quarter of the population is employed in growing wheat, maize, potatoes, olives, grapes, citrus fruits, figs, spring vegetables and onions.

At the same time, fishing for sardines, cod and tuna is more important than the raising of cattle, pigs or sheep. The Portuguese have had to struggle with many different problems in the agricultural industry. Its portion of the gross national product has decreased considerably from 33% in 1950 to under 11% in 1986. After the Revolution of 1910 many great landowners were dispossessed, which resulted in a decided decrease in production, due to the inadequately organised co-operatives, but many of these measures have now been withdrawn.

The Industrial scene
While agriculture is somewhat in decline, industry on the other hand is making really good progress. Most activity is concentrated around the harbours of Lisbon, Oporto and Sines, and also in Minho Province. Foodstuffs and textiles, together with the processing of wood and cork, still play the biggest roles, and the majority of the labour force is employed in these industries. Mechanical engineering and the electrical and pharmaceutical industries are relatively new ventures now showing signs of profitability.

In industrial areas the standard of living is relatively high. The district of Lisbon, including the rural areas of Estremadura, brings in half of the total tax return for the whole of the country, in spite of the fact that the population is just under one fifth of the total. 39% of the cars and 43% of all television sets are found in this region. Portugal is fortunate in having at its disposal a considerable amount of mineral resources. The most important of these are uranium, the deposits of which are second in size only to those of France, together with pyrites, iron, manganese, tungsten, zinc and lead. Most of the ores which are mined cannot be processed in the country and are exported in their raw state. The Portuguese have, for several years, been trying to set up a productive steel industry in and around Lisbon.

Energy
Things are not quite so healthy in the energy sector. The country has no oil deposits and the only coal worth mining is on the coast between Oporto and Figueira da Foz. This is relatively insignificant and is sufficient only for the supply to a few power stations. At the present time, Portugal's consistently increasing demand for energy is served mainly by water power.

Looking to the future, the existing electricity capacity will be by no means sufficient, but the rich deposits of uranium offer a solution to the problem, and several nuclear power stations are planned.

Cork oaks

Tourism

Tourism plays a vital role in the government's plans for the further development of the economy. Between 1974 and 1976 tourism declined, but it is now once again on the increase, although a degree of caution has been exercised as regards the building of hotels. Only on the Algarve has the coast been developed on a really massive scale. Approximately half the foreign tourists come from Spain. The remainder are mostly English, Germans, French and Americans.

Transport

The transport system is still in the stage of development. Of the 3,500 km of railway network, nearly 800 km are still narrow gauge, which causes big problems where goods traffic is involved. Railway electrification has been in progress, however, for some years. Portugal's road system is some 35,000 km long and is generally in good condition. The country still has no long-distance motorways, but parts of the Lisbon/Oporto route have been completed. The most important forms of public transport are the trains and buses. An underground railway operates in the capital and local transport works smoothly in the remaining towns. Portuguese navigation has a great tradition, but the number of ships sailing under the Portuguese flag has decreased around the world. To compensate for this, the state airline, TAP (Air Portugal), has had an increase in passengers. The airport in Lisbon is developing into a centre for traffic between Europe, South America and West Africa.

Signposts of History

From 10,000 B.C.: First settlements in the land which is now Portugal.

About 2,000 B.C.: Iberian peoples, probably from North Africa, settle in the peninsula south of the Pyrenees.

From 700 B.C.: Settlement by the Celtic tribes of Lusitania which gave the land its name.

179 B.C.: Lusitania unites with the Roman province of *Hispania Ulterior*.

A.D. 410: The West Goths and other Germanic tribes invade the Iberian peninsula. The Roman Empire falls.

711: The Moors conquer the whole area as far as the Douro. Small Christian kingdoms in the north begin to reconquer their land - the *Reconquista*.

1095: Henry of Burgundy reigns over *Portucalia*, a region between Minho and the River Tagus.

1139: Henry's son, Afonso, wins a great battle against the Moors and proclaims himself king.

1249: The conquest of Faro. The Moslems are expelled and the country has now reached its current dimensions.

1279: Dinis, the peasant king, establishes the State and founds a university at Coimbra.

1368: Following war with Castile, Portugal forms an alliance with England which has lasted until the present day.

1415: Conquest of Ceuta. Prince Henry the Navigator organises systematic voyages of discovery along the African coast.

1497: Vasco da Gama discovers the sea route to India.

1500: Pedro Alvarez Cabral discovers Brazil.

1520: Portugal obtains a foothold in Goa, in the Moluccas, Java, Ceylon and in China.

1580: The Empire falls after invasion by Spain. 60 years of foreign rule.

1700: Gold rush in Brazil encouraging emigration. The people become more and more impoverished. The economic dependence on England increases.

1750: The Marquês of Pombal attempts unsuccessfully to introduce reforms.

1822: Brazil becomes independent and Portugal's financial position deteriorates.

1910: The bankruptcy of the State seems unavoidable. Revolution. Portugal a republic. The first successes of the new government are hindered by the outbreak of the First World War.

1926: Military coup. Salazar becomes Finance Minister and, in 1932, Prime Minister. He rules as a dictator and in 1968 is succeeded by Caetano.

1974: Bloodless revolution. Democracy restored.

1986: Under Mário Soares Portugal joins the EEC.

Abbey of Batalha

Phases of History

Portuguese history is not only the story of intrepid colonisers and navigators, but also of an heroic struggle for the political independence of this small country. Here is a brief account of the most important events in the history of Portugal.

The Reconquest

It may sound strange but the true history of an independent Portugal has to begin with its occupation by a foreign power. In the year A.D. 711 the Moors defeated Roderich, king of the Western Goths, at the *Battle of Guadalete* and proceeded to occupy almost the whole of the Iberian peninsula. They held the areas around Santarem and Lisbon until 1147, and it was not until 1240 that the Algarve was finally liberated.

In 717 the period of the *Reconquista* began, when the Christians set about reconquering their country from the Moors, eventually forming the Portuguese Empire. In 1128 Dom Afonso Henriques assumed the role of king, freed his country from Spain and expelled the Moors, but even after his final victory over Islam the young nation was unable to find peace. The constant wars with Castile ended temporarily in 1385 when King João won the *Battle of Aljubarrota*. To commemorate this victory the king erected the splendid Abbey of Batalha.

The Empire

The third son of João was Henriques, better known as Henry the Navigator, who was one of Portugal's most famous sons. With the capture of Ceuta in Morocco in 1415

Henry began the period of Portuguese conquests and discoveries. The island groups of Madeira and the Azores, already recorded on ancient maps, were rediscovered; Senegal, the Gambia and the islands of São Tome and Fernando Pô in the Gulf of Guinea were also discovered. Naval captains, trained by Henry the Navigator in Sagres on the Algarve, crossed the Equator in 1417. Under King João II Bartolomeu Diaz reached the Cape of Good Hope and in 1492 Labrador was discovered. King Manuel I made Portugal one of the greatest colonial powers of the time. Vasco da Gama discovered the sea route to India (1497–99), and part of the subcontinent was later colonised by Portugal. In 1500 Alvarez Cabral took possession of Brazil for Portugal. The discoveries and conquests continued; Goa, the Moluccas and Ceylon were occupied and Portuguese soldiers set foot on Chinese soil. In 1519 Magellan was the first man to sail round the world - albeit in Spanish ships - and under King João III (1521–47) the Portuguese reached Japan.

Occupation by Spain

In 1580 the Cardinal-King Henriques died without leaving a successor, and the prosperity of Portugal faded. Taking advantage of the vacant throne, King Philip II of Spain invaded and occupied the country. During the time of the Spanish occupation, Portugal lost many of its colonial gains to Holland. In 1640 the nobility, under the leader who later became King João IV, rose up against the Spaniards and with Dutch assistance regained their country. At the same time, Brazilian soldiers recaptured Angola and São Tomé. Portugal was regaining its might and its wealth.

The Carnation Revolution

In more recent times, Portugal has had a rather gloomy record. From 1926 to 1974 a Fascist military dictator ruled in Lisbon. In no other country was Fascism able to keep a hold for such a long period. The oppression brought to Portugal by the generals was eventually overthrown by the more junior officers in the army who re-established democracy in the country.

On April 25th 1974 tanks rolled through the streets of Lisbon, occupying all the most strategic positions. So unexpected was this military coup that it was successful without a shot being fired. The soldiers wore red carnations on their uniforms as a sign of their left-wing democratic views, which gave the coup its name, and they were greeted with the greatest enthusiasm by the people.

As the first euphoria subsided, however, it became apparent that the change from dictatorship to democracy was not going to be an easy matter. There was a renewed attempt by General Antonio de Spinola to overthrow the democratic government, but the coup failed and Spinola was forced to flee to Brazil. Economic problems now beset the country, causing strikes and violent clashes between left-wing farmworkers and the great landowners in Alentejo. But the 'floral revolution' had not been for nothing. Since 1976 Portugal has enjoyed a stable parliamentary democracy. Since 1987 the PSD (Partida Socialista Democrata) has been in power under the leadership of Cavaco Silver.

Roman mosaics at Conimbriga

Two thousand years of Art

It must be said immediately that relics of the Roman occupation or of the settlement of Germanic tribes are few and far between in Portugal. It is true that there are many wonderful artefacts in the country's archaeological museums but in general there are few monuments or edifices dating back to pre-Roman times. The two most splendid examples of ancient architecture on Portuguese soil are the Pillars of the Temple of Diana in Evora (3rd–2nd c. B.C.), and the Roman mosaics of *Conimbriga* near Coimbra.

In spite of their long presence in Portugal, the Moors did not leave behind them as much imposing architecture as they did in Spanish Andalusia. The influence of Islamic art is, however, quite unmistakable, especially in the south — in motifs on ornaments, in oriental arches and columns and in the frequent use of blue or other brightly coloured tiles. In Portugal, buildings of the Romanesque period nearly always show evidence of the Gothic style which followed it, in the shape of transitional or mixed architectural forms. The immense cathedral at Coimbra still exhibits a fairly pure form of Romanesque, whilst the old cathedrals at Braga (the first great Romanesque building in Portugal), Lisbon, Évora and Oporto had Gothic and other elements added later, producing a mixture of styles. The purest form of Gothic architecture and, at the same time, one of the most magnificent buildings in Portugal, is Santa Maria de Vitória in Batalha. Works by the famous Portuguese artist Nuno Gonçalves were painted in the Gothic period and his masterpiece, the polyptych from St Vincent's altar, still hangs today in the Museum of Ancient Art in Lisbon.

Braga — the Garden at St Barbara

Manueline Art

In the age of discovery, an independent form of Portuguese art, known as *Manueline*, after King Manuel I, emerged from the late Gothic period. The maritime success of Henry the Navigator and his men, together with the impressions provided by the recently discovered New World, gave inspiration to the Manueline style, with its designs portraying hawsers, sailors' knots and various sorts of seaweed, and with the use of trinkets and botanical specimens from Africa, South America and the Far East.

The best-known of these Portuguese national styles can be seen in the works of the master-builders and sculptors, Diego and Francisco de Arruda, João de Castilho, Mateus Fernandes (father and son), and of Boytac, also known as Boytaca, who came from France. Their work includes the Hieronymus Monastery of Belém in Lisbon, the unfinished Sepulchre Chapels of Batalha, parts of the Church of the Knights of Christ in Tomar, and the Royal Palace in Sintra. Outside Portugal Manueline architecture can only be found in a few places in Brazil.

Renaissance architecture

The Renaissance in Portugal was strongly influenced by the French and Italians, and their styles were often adopted by the national builders and artists. Some of the better-known examples of their work can be found at Évora, Tomar and Coimbra. Buildings in the Baroque style are distinguished by the way that they tone in with their surroundings. With a few exceptions they are not as highly decorated as the German nor as monumental as the Italian Baroque. The magnificent monastery in Mafra, the country seat of Queluz near Lisbon and the Clérigos Church in Oporto are the most outstanding examples of Baroque architecture in Portugal. 18th-century Baroque in the churches is characterised by the use of carved and heavily gilded walls, ceilings and altar furnishings, known as *Talha Dourada*. Beautiful examples of this style can be found in Santo António Church in Lagos and in the Church of Santa Clara in Oporto. The methodical rebuilding of the Lower Town of Lisbon, with its huge plaza, Praça do Comércio, following the massive earthquake of 1755, serves as a typical example of civic architecture.

Azulejos ornamentation

In Portugal tiles, known as *azulejos*, white and blue at first but later of varying colours, have played a very important role in design since the 15th c. Coloured tiles, some with geometric patterns and others with pictures painted on them, were used in churches for decoration as well as in palaces and stately homes, both inside and outside the building. These tiles came in the first place from Holland and Spain, and were subsequently produced in Portugal itself. In the 17th and 18th centuries in particular they were extensively used, even in gardens and as decoration on fountains. Especially attractive examples of this form of art can be found, among other places, at Évora, Lisbon, Faro and Beja (monastery museum).

The art of gold- and silversmiths has always been highly regarded in Portugal. An outstanding masterpiece is the sacramental altar in Oporto Cathedral; several silversmiths took 100 years to complete this work.

Left: Traditional azulejos tiles. Right: Hieronymus monastery, Belém

Food and Drink

Portugal's culinary art deserves much greater recognition. Of course, the hotel menus can make tedious reading, as they can in most countries. Half board is therefore preferable to full board and is, in many ways, more convenient.

To the gourmet, Portuguese cooking appears to be very 'Spanish' and, in fact, the close relationship with Andalusian cuisine cannot be denied. Like the Spanish, the Portuguese cook mainly with olive oil, but in larger quantities. Garlic is also a common ingredient used in the home. As in neighbouring Spain, meals in Portuguese restaurants can be sumptuous.

Tourist hotels offer most types of international cuisine but you should not be afraid to visit a specialist restaurant. Here, for example, you can find on the menu:

Soup *(Sopa)*
Caldo verde: a tasty soup made from cabbage.
Sopa Alentejana: an unusual combination of meat stock, olive oil and poached egg, seasoned with garlic and chervil.
Creme de mariscos: a broth made from mussels.
Gaspacho: an ice-cold soup with raw puréed tomatoes, cucumbers and paprika. A true Andalusian speciality.

Fish and shellfish *(Peixe e Mariscos)*
Lulas: squid, prepared in various ways.
Bacalhau: the Portuguese national dish - dried cod. There are supposed to be 365 different ways in which to prepare it. At Christmas time it is the traditional dish, boiled and basted with vinegar and oil and eaten by rich and poor alike.
Amêijoas: the Portuguese term for mussels, which each region prepares in its own special way.
Lagosta: lobster, which is at its best as 'Lagosta Grelhada' - grilled with a butter sauce.

Meat dishes *(Carne)*
Carne de porco à Alentejana: a 'hybrid' - pork and mussels stewed together.
Gabrito: goat meat, usually braised in oil together with tomatoes and seasoned with garlic.
Febras de porco: charcoal-grilled pork cutlets.
Dobrada: a typical dish but not to everyone's taste. A hot-pot of offal cooked in a lot of oil and garlic with spicy sausage, pieces of chicken and large white beans.
Leitão Assado: grilled sucking pig.
Cozido: boiled beef with sausage. Various vegetables *(legumes)*, and potatoes *(batata)* or rice *(arroz)* can be added to the main dish.
Iscas: pickled liver - a Portuguese speciality. Sliced calves' liver, marinated for several hours in vinegar, salt, pepper, bay leaves and garlic; quickly browned and the marinade then poured over it.

Caldeirade (fish stew)

One of several methods of preparation: place some fish heads, a sliced onion and a bay leaf in water, white wine and lemon juice. Bring to the boil and then strain the stock. Slice two peeled onions and a clove of garlic. Fry in oil until transparent and then add peeled tomatoes, parsley and coriander. Top up with the stock. Clean and prepare pieces of cod and lightly cook in the prepared fish stock adding, according to taste and pocket, some washed mussels and pieces of shelled crab and lobster. Season with salt, pepper and sweet paprika and simmer until tender. Pour into a tureen, garnish with chopped parsley and serve with pieces of white bread.

Desserts *(Sobremesas)*

The desserts or sweets *(doces)* which are available are many and varied — numerous sorts of puddings *(pudim)*, every type of pastry *(bolo)*, and unusual combinations such as *Castanhada* (a mixture of chestnut purée, sugar and egg yolk). Fruit is abundant according to season. Oranges *(laranja)*, melons *(melão)*, grapes *(uvas)*, strawberries *(morangos)* and peaches *(pêssego)*. There is not, however, a great variety of cheeses *(queijo)*.

Breakfast *(Pequeno Almoco)*

Coffee *(café)* is usually good but tea *(chá)* is also available. If you like egg dishes, you can order *ovo quente* (poached egg), *ovo mexido* (scrambled egg), *ovo estrelado* (fried egg) or omelette, which comes in either the usual form *(omoleta)* or prepared in the Spanish style *(tortilla)*.

Drinks *(Bebidas)*

Portugal is a wine country. *Vinho tinto* is red wine, *vinho branco* white wine. Almost every region produces its own wine, usually light and nourishing, from the barrel *(vinho regional* and *vinho da casa)* .

Of course in the wine country of Portugal you can also get a cool glass of pale ale. The local beer is called *Cerveja* and is very good. The *Super Bock* is perhaps the best, but it can only be found in the north. The best-known brands are *Skol* and *Sagres*.

As the Portuguese diet is so oily, it might be advisable after a meal to settle the stomach with a glass of brandy *(aguardente)*. The best brandy for this purpose is *Bagaço*, made from similar grapes to those used for the Italian grappa. Portuguese brandies are excellent. A *Constantinho* is sometimes preferred to a good French cognac. Other good brands are *1902, Antigua,* and *Macieira*.

Non-alcoholic drinks include first-class fruit juices and healthy, palatable mineral waters.

Guide to Wine

The famous port wine from the Oporto region is a full-bodied fortified wine, usually red in colour, extremely dark or with a yellow sheen and is at its best as a vintage wine. Less frequently do you see white port. From the north of Coimbra comes *Dão*, which is like a burgundy and can be either red or white. In the Lisbon region *Bucelas* is produced, a semi-dry light red or white wine.

Next to port, *Vinho Verde* from the Minho province is the best known of Portuguese wines. The 'green wine' is a refreshing, slightly sparkling, red or white wine which can be dry or semi-sweet. Made from a special type of grape, picked before it is fully ripe, Vinho Verde stands out against all others as a really excellent wine. The Minho region is renowned in addition for its sparkling, semi-dry rosé wines, Mateus being the most popular and well known.

The light white or red *Bairada* wines which come from the areas around Aveiro or Coimbra are rather dry, while the Algarve produces the medium-strength, usually red, Lagoa wines. If you like a full-bodied table wine, try *Romeira* (red) or *Piriquita* (white). Surprisingly good are the *Espumantes*, the Portuguese sparkling wines; the ones in greatest demand are *Raposeira* and *Messias*.

Holidays in Portugal

When considering the reasons why you should go to Portugal for a holiday, there are so many possibilities that it is sometimes difficult to make the right choice. Below you will find a brief account of what you may expect to find in Portugal and what there is to do there, which may help you to make the right decisions as to the best region to visit, the most suitable holiday resort, the right type of accommodation, the best season of the year and the excursions which are the most appropriate to your needs.

If you want a completely individual holiday free from stress then you should go in winter to the south Portuguese Atlantic coast, the Algarve, with its lonely beaches, very pleasant temperatures and little wind. Bathing in the sea is advisable only between May and November, unless you are an extremely hardy person, but there are excellent heated swimming pools available. It is also a good idea to visit the Algarve when the almond trees are in blossom in February or at Easter. In the summer some places can become rather overcrowded. Northern Portugal is more for those wanting to learn about the country and its people, rather than looking for a perfect holiday centre. It is cheaper here and there are fewer foreign tourists, but this is the real Portugal. A word of warning though: even in summer the water temperature can be relatively low and August temperatures can sometimes reach 'only' 18°C.

Lisbon, Estoril and Cascais appeal to those gregarious holidaymakers who like being with people and who enjoy the milling throng. There is always something going on in these places.

Holidays with children

You can also travel confidently in Portugal with children, provided that you consider carefully beforehand where you wish to go. Only a few resorts are really geared for children and several stretches of beach with their strong Atlantic breakers are just not suitable for the 5- or 6-year old. You will find in this guide information on the most suitable places for children, but, as in all Latin countries, youngsters are never considered to be a nuisance.

Right: Gathering grapes for Vinho Verde

🎭 Special entertainment

Do you want more than the usual 'ethnic' shows put on just for the tourists? Your wishes can be fulfilled in Portugal. More so than in other countries, church festivals *(festas)* and pilgrimages *(romarias)*, often lasting all day, are still celebrated in traditional style in many places. A very special type of entertainment is the bullfight *(tourada)* which in Portugal is bloodless. Naturally most bullfights are held in Lisbon, but genuine Portuguese bullfights can be seen even in the smaller towns, where they take place in the most makeshift of arenas, even in the market place!

🛌 🏃 Relaxation — Sport and Games

If you want a holiday geared to your health Portugal does not offer the same facilities as Romania or northern Italy. Nevertheless there are nineteen thermal spas, although they are not particularly well known internationally. The climate in Portugal is healthy; the air, especially in the mountains, is very pure and the sea is rich in iodine and trace elements. If you set out, not in search of a rigid health regime, but just to take it easy and 'recharge the batteries', then in Portugal you will sleep, walk and breathe in the most relaxed fashion. Many people go in for sport with health in mind, and there are plenty of opportunities for an active holiday all the year round. Golf and tennis are extremely popular, while for those who like riding there are plenty of horses available. For the angler, fishing in the rivers, from rocks and out at sea makes this country an angler's paradise. Small fish, large fish, all sizes abound, from herrings to sharks. The rocky coastline is ideal for snorkelers and divers. Surfing is limited to protected bays owing to the very strong breakers. Water-skiing, sailing and riding are not possible in all the holiday resorts, but relevant information will be found later on in this guide under the name of the place concerned.

Football is just as popular in Portugal as bullfighting. You can go quite happily to a premier league match as there is virtually no hooliganism. In spite of enormous enthusiasm the public is very disciplined.

🛍 Shopping and souvenirs

When you are on holiday it is inevitable that you spend more money than you do at home, and a shopping spree is really part of the holiday. Certainly you will rarely find such curious or unusual souvenirs in Portugal as you would in Africa or Asia, but there are plenty of attractive little gifts to take home. If you understand something about them, interesting and above all genuine antiques can be found. Don't look for them, however, in the main streets of the big cities or in the international seaside resorts, but in the more out-of-the-way streets and smaller towns and villages.

In addition, you can buy jewellery, embroidery, leather goods and, particularly, pottery. More attractive tiles, for instance, cannot be found anywhere else. Some items of clothing, such as jeans, are much cheaper here and those bearing the 'Wrangler' or 'Levi's' label are quite often 'made in Portugal'.

Why not also take back vintage port or madeira, as you would pay much more at home. Other local spirits, brandies and liqueurs are excellent and good value. Here is a tip — don't ever buy in the first shop you go into. Compare the prices; the same goods are often cheaper down the road!

Holidays in Portugal

Top left: Bullfighting — bloodless in Portugal

Top right: Leather goods — souvenirs from Minho Province

Bottom right: Ceramic souvenirs

Above: Fishermen wait for the tide

Hints for your holiday

This guide covers every type of holiday which you may wish to take. Specialist information on such subjects as the history of art is not specifically included, but certain tips are given which are not always found in travel guides. Here are just a few hints which can help make your holiday the most enjoyable part of the year.

'When in Portugal...'

Learn a few words of Portuguese — 'thank you', 'please', 'good morning' and 'good bye' would be quite a good beginning.

Portugal is too beautiful and too varied a country for you to remain in one resort all the time. Wherever you are, a trip to Lisbon should not be missed, as it is one of the most splendid cities in the world.

If you travel independently to Portugal it is quite easy to find good accommodation. *Pousadas* offer genuine Portuguese cuisine in attractive surroundings but it is necessary to book early.

In Portugal itself, as well as in the pages of this guide, you will frequently come across these three terms:

Miradouro — the term used for vantage points. They are usually indicated by means of a sign and it is worth looking out for them.

Azulejos — the blue and colourful tiles which are used for all sorts of decoration. Some are made up into ornaments and others are used to make murals.

Pelourinho — a medieval whipping post. Often highly decorated and usually to be found in the town square.

A tip for water fanatics: apart from in sheltered bays special caution must be exercised when swimming. In most places, especially on the west coast, there are large breakers, strong currents and a powerful undertow. And the water is cooler than in the Mediterranean.

Where to go and what to see

Lisbon

'Quem não viu Lisboa, não viu coisa boa' (anyone who has not seen Lisbon has not seen anything worth while). This old proverb still holds good today. With a population of about 900,000, Lisbon is one of the smaller European capitals, but certainly among the finest. The most westerly and, next to Athens, the most southerly capital in Europe, it lies on a bay at the mouth of the River Tagus. This bay, which is known as the *Mar de Palha* and which at this point is almost 10 km wide, reveals Lisbon in the most dramatic way. The mighty steel bridge which spans the river and is over 2½ km long is known as the *Ponte 25 de Abril* and is the largest suspension bridge in Europe. It connects the capital to the suburbs of Cacilhas and Almada which lie on the other side of the Tagus. Like Rome Lisbon was built on seven hills, and is spread out along the northern bank of the river, with its white or pastel-coloured houses nestling on the slopes and in the valleys.

Monument to the Discoveries

History

After the Reconquista (the Reconquest) by King Afonso I in 1147, Lisbon was the epicentre of the young Portuguese nation, the point from which the age of world-wide exploration and conquest was begun. From the metropolis on the Tagus, Vasco da Gama set sail for India.

In 1755 disaster struck and the flourishing capital was almost wiped out. A tremendous earthquake, accompanied by fires which raged for several days, and an almighty tidal wave from the estuary of the Tagus left most of Lisbon in ruins. More than 40,000 people were killed. However, thanks to the initiative of the then Secretary of State, the Marquês de Pombal, Portugal's capital was rebuilt on a grand scale.

 ## Sightseeing

There is something for everybody in Lisbon, whether the intention is just to look around, to see something in particular or to go in for a sporting activity.

The City centre

The best place to start from when exploring the capital is the *Praça do Comércio*. This square, which lies on the bank of the River Tagus, is lined with long stretches of buildings, with covered walkways, and dominated by the equestrian statue of King José I. From here, most of the places of interest in Lisbon can be reached quite comfortably on foot. Three streets, parallel to each other, lead to the town centre, the *Rossio*. All three are very popular shopping areas for tourists and residents alike. The finest is the *Rua Augusta*, which is approached through a triumphal arch.

The Rossio — its official name of *Praça Dom Pedro* is hardly known even by Lisbon drivers — is the centre of social

Left: Rossio Square, Lisbon

Ponte 25 de Abril

life. In the middle of this busy square the smiling King Dom Pedro looks down from his column on the bustling confusion below, street traders, newspaper sellers, shoe cleaners, lottery ticket vendors, all shouting their wares and mingling with the passing throng. The *Praça dos Restauradores*, with its 30-m-high obelisk commemorating the liberation from foreign Spanish rule in the 17th c., is quite close to the Classical theatre, *Dona Maria II*. The Portuguese tourist office is situated in the *Palácio Foz*.

From there to the *Praça Marquês de Pombal* stretches the *Avenida da Liberdade* which is 1½ km long and 100 m wide. This avenue, with its mosaic pavements, street cafés, theatres, cinemas and top-class hotels, must surely be Lisbon's most attractive thoroughfare. Behind it extends the immense *Parque Eduardo VII* (covering 160,000 sq. m), which was laid out at the beginning of the 20th c. on the occasion of an official visit to Lisbon by King Edward VII. From the highest point of the square, a very good view of the city centre can be obtained. The principal feature of the park is the *Estufa Fria*, a large glasshouse containing a wide variety of tropical plants.

Chiado quarter and Bairro Alto

Visible from afar and towering over the *Chiado quarter* are the ruins of the *Igreja do Carmo* (the Carmelite Church). Only the pillars and the transverse

Castelo de São Jorge

View over the Alfama and harbour

arches survived the earthquake of 1755. The open-air archaeological museum *(Museu Arqueologia)* has been formed around these ruins. The Chiado quarter, most easily reached by the *Elevador de Santa Justa*, a lift which was installed in 1901 by Gustave Eiffel, is the most elegant place to shop in the area. The main streets, *Rua Garrett* and *Rua Serpa Pinto*, in which stands the Museum of Contemporary Art *(Museu Nacional de Arte Contemporânea)*, lead to the lovely *Largo do Chiado*, the central part of the quarter.

The adjacent *Bairra Alto* owes its reputation to the taverns where the fado is performed, as well as to its smaller inexpensive restaurants, which are mostly to be found in the *Rua da Rosa* and the *Rua Barroca*. You can, if you wish, come here to listen to the ancient Portuguese folk music which is still played and sung even to this day.

Alfama, Sé and Castelo de São Jorge

That part of the city known as *Alfama* is the oldest district of Lisbon, the historical birthplace of the city. A tortuous thread of narrow streets, alleyways and steps winds its way up to the Castelo de São Jorge past windows with washing draped in front, curious little shops, raucous bars, noisy children at play and public washing places.

The Alfama is the most lively and attractive part of the city. It is an area which boasts many historically interesting buildings and churches. You should not miss a visit to at least one of the three small 13thc. churches which have survived, such as the *Igreja São Estevão*. The capacity for interest in the Alfama is almost inexhaustible and days could be spent here. The two most famous buildings are, without doubt, the *Sé Patriacal* (the cathedral) and the *Castelo de São Jorge*. The Sé was erected in the 12th c. as a Romanesque fortress and, as a result of several

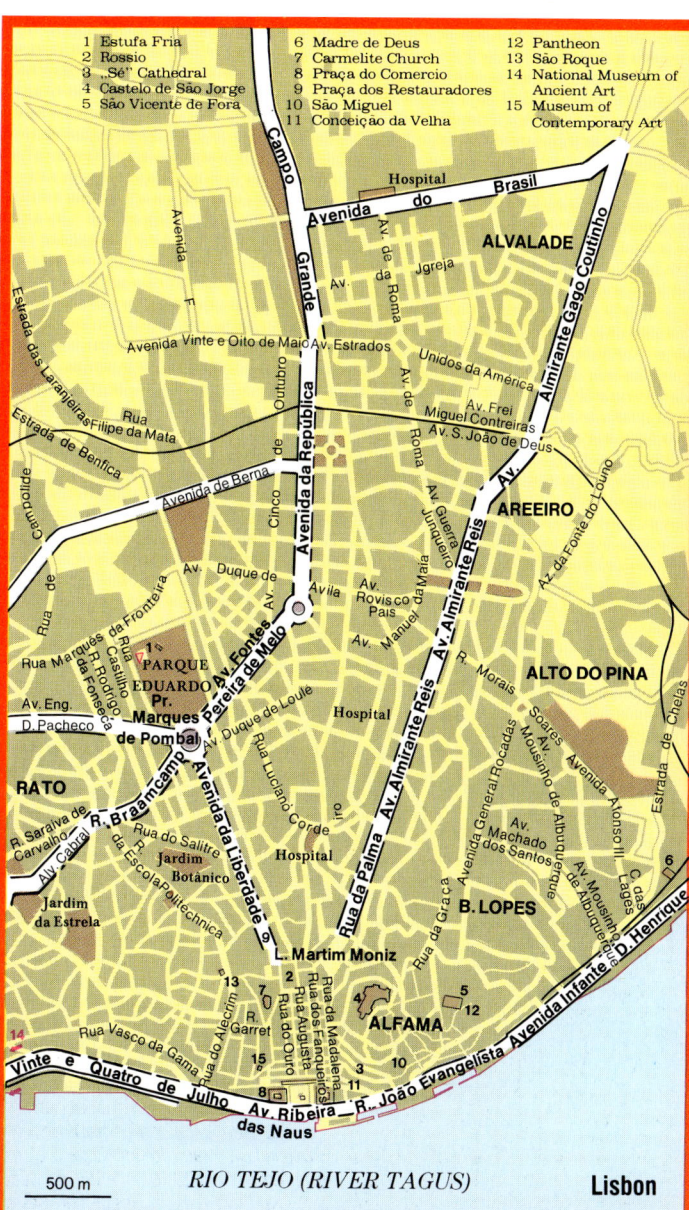

earthquakes, has been rebuilt in several architectural styles. Today, the interior is still largely Romanesque and it is worth a visit if only to see the 14th c. cloisters and the *Bartolomeu Joanes* side chapel.

The Castelo de São Jorge was also repeatedly reduced to ruins and the extensive castle grounds shared a similar fate, but the fortress was always reconstructed, each time on a larger scale. It was for several centuries the seat of the Portuguese kings, but today it serves as the finest vantage point from which to view the capital.

Belém

Belém, the residential suburb of Lisbon which has developed from the former port of *Restelo*, is the capital's second largest tourist centre. Two great examples of Manueline architecture stand here. The *Mosteiro dos Jeronimós* (the Hieronymus Monastery) was commissioned by King Manuel I at the beginning of the 16th c.; the transept which was created by Castilho is an architectural wonder. The *Torre de Belém*, which was once a lighthouse and constructed in the time of Manuel I,

Below: Cloisters of the Hieronymus monastery. Right: Torre de Belém

is the most photographed building in Portugal. Next to it you can find an excellent example of modern sculpture, the *Padrão dos Descobrimentos* (Monument to the Discoveries), which dates from 1959 and depicts the prow of a sailing vessel.

In addition Belém is the home of three museums, all of which are worth a visit. The Museum of Popular Art *(Museu de Arte Popular)* gives a comprehensive view of art, costumes and customs throughout the provinces; in the Marine Museum *(Museu da Marinha)* there are models of ships spanning six centuries. The unparalleled National Museum of Carriages *(Museu Nacional dos Coches)*, situated in the former stables of the old castle, houses the largest collection of carriages and state coaches in the world; they are well worth seeing.

Other churches

Basilica de Estrela. This late Baroque basilica, built in the 18th c. from white Alcântara marble, is one of Lisbon's landmarks. There is a wonderful view of the city from the dome and adjacent to the church is a small park, the *Parque da Estrela*.

Caso dos Bicos

Igreja da Madre de Deus. Founded as a monastery at the beginning of the 16th c., the whole of the building was completely destroyed in 1755 but it was later rebuilt in the reign of King José I. In the Tile Museum *(Museu dos Azulejos)*, situated in part of the former monastery, over 10,000 tiles, going back six centuries, are on display.

Igreja São Roque. This church was built at the end of the 16th c. under the direction of the master builder Filippo Terzi. Apart from the beautiful Renaissance interior, the side chapel of *São João Baptista*, dating from the 18th c., is of considerable interest.

Igreja São Vincente de Fora. Modelled by Filippo Terzi on the Il Gesù Church in Rome, the interior of this building is mainly in the Baroque style; the High Altar by Machado de Castro is particularly noteworthy.

Secular buildings

Aqueduto das Águas Livres. This Baroque-style aqueduct was begun in 1728. The tallest of the 35 arches is 65 m high and the aqueduct is a kilometre in length.

Caso dos Bicos. This old 16th c. palace was partly destroyed in 1755. The façade, which still remains, is of ashlar masonry, every other stone being diamond-shaped.

Pantheon. Work began on this church at the end of the 17th c. but was not completed until 250 years later. Inside can be found the *Kenotaphe*, a large monument commemorating the deaths of famous Portuguese who are buried elsewhere, including Vasco da Gama, Henry the Navigator, Albuquerque and the poet Camoēs.

Museums

Among the 30 or more museums in Lisbon, apart from those already mentioned, the following are of particular interest:

Museu da Fundação Caluste Gulbenkian. The most important departments of this museum contain art collections of Eastern, Armenian, Greek and Egyptian origin, as well as works by the better-known European artists. The large collection of porcelain is famous.

Museu Nacional de Arte Antiqua. The *National Museum of Ancient Art* is best known for its collection of paintings by foreign and Portuguese artists. Other departments in the museum are notable for goldsmiths' work, tapestries and ceramics.

Museu Nacional de Arqueologia e Etnografia. The *National Archaeological and Ethnological Museum* in Belém is worth a visit by anyone interested in pre-Roman history, which is very well represented. The ceramics and the intricate work of goldsmiths are also deserving of attention.

Museu de Artilharia. In this military museum you can see armour and weaponry dating back six centuries. Definitely a must for enthusiasts.

Parks

Jardim Botánico. The *Botanical Gardens* are one of the loveliest places in Lisbon, with exotic plants from South America, Asia and Africa.

Jardim Zoológico. A zoo, with good restaurants and well laid out gardens.

Parque Florestal de Monsanto. In this, the largest park in the city, there are numerous restaurants as well as sports facilities of all kinds and several good vantage points.

Fado singers in the Alfama

Entertainment

You will not find the same variety of entertainment in the Portuguese metropolis as in other European capitals. Nevertheless, there are numerous theatre, opera and operetta productions, some of which are performed in the open air *(the Rossio)*, although they usually take place in modern cultural centres such as the *Fundação Caluste Gulbenkian*. Every visitor to Lisbon should patronise, at least once, the famous fado saloons in the *Bairro Alto* suburb of the city. The traditional folk music can be heard from 11 p.m. onwards.

The bloodless Portuguese bullfight takes place in the *Arena Campo Pequeno* from July to September inclusive.

Food and drink

Almost every type of Portuguese speciality can be found in Lisbon. Fish is plentiful and is the best value for money. Many of the best restaurants are concentrated in the *Rua das Portas de Santo Antão*.

Around Lisbon

Seaside resorts and fishing villages

Lisbon itself does not have any beaches, but the well known resorts of Estoril and Cascais may easily be reached from the capital by high-speed railway.

Estoril (25 km west) is an elegant luxury health resort with grand hotels, thermal baths, golf courses and a casino.

Cascais (3 km further on) was for a long time a popular place of exile for dethroned monarchs and banished heads of state. This former fishing village is today renowned for its numerous gourmet restaurants, the speciality of which is the locally produced lobster. Between them Estoril and Cascais, with their long sandy beaches which stretch for miles, provide all the comforts necessary for a modern holiday. Not only all forms of water sport, but also tennis, golf and riding are available.

Ericeira (57 km north-west) has developed from a picturesque fishing village to a very popular holiday centre, with its beaches encircled by cliffs, and its excellent restaurants.

Costa da Caparica (13 km south) lies on the other side of the Tagus. The town, which is visited mainly by the Portuguese, is not terribly attractive. This does not apply to the beaches, however. Situated at the edge of a vast pine forest, they stretch for over 30 km and are among the longest in Europe.

Mafra Monastery

🚌 Places to visit

Queluz (12km north-west). In the middle of a delightful park laid out on a grand scale stands the *Palácio Nacional*, a royal castle built in the Rococo style and dating from the 18th c., but which is not open to the public.

Sintra (25 km north-west). This little town, with its two palaces, is one of the most popular tourist attractions in Portugal. The *Palácio Real* (14th to 16th c.) is a good example of the Eastern influence on so many of Portugal's buildings. Its two enormous chimneys are landmarks in this photogenic provincial township. Nearby is the *Palácio da Pena*, an ugly 19th c. folly

Peniche

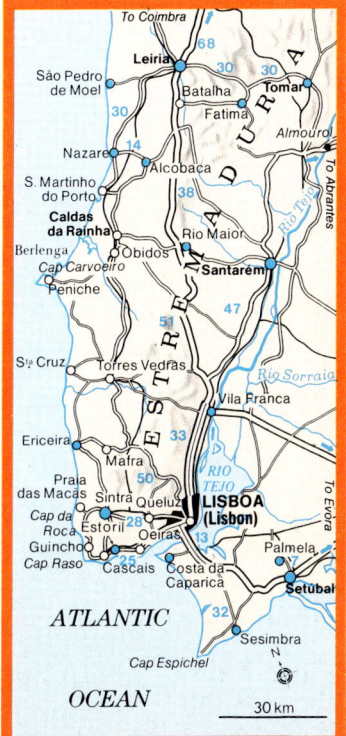

made up of every architectural style imaginable. In addition there is the *Parque de Monserrate*, an extensive botanical garden with many of the unusual plants which are to be found in the region.

Mafra (45 km north). The monastery here is the largest building in the country, constructed at the beginning of the 18th c. and covering an area of 40,000 sq. metres. The monastery chapel, containing reliefs by Machado de Castro, the library, housing more than 35,000 books, and the carillon, which originated in Antwerp, are all of particular interest.

Palmela (41 km south). The large castle of Palmela was built in the time of the Moorish occupation. It was extended in the 17th and 18th centuries and is today a pousada.

Setúbal (48 km south). This is Portugal's largest fishing port. Towering above the town is the *Castel de São Filipe* (pousada), while in the centre are two very interesting churches, *São Julião*, with its fine example of a Manueline doorway, and the 15th c. *Igreja de Jesus*; both are worth a visit.

Sesimbra (32 km south). Sesimbra lies on the slopes of the *Serra de Arrábida*, and there is a wonderful view from the well preserved ramparts of the 17th c. fortress.

The Algarve landscape

The word 'Algarve' comes from the Arabic meaning 'The West'. The region is sometimes referred to as the Algarve coast, but in reality it has much more to offer than just a stretch of coastline. In fact, the coast itself may be divided into two quite different parts but, strictly speaking, there are four types of scenery in the Algarve: the rugged coast with its unusual rock formations, the sandy beaches, the garden region, and finally the mountains.

Climate

All four types of region have some things in common, however, including the southern climate which is agreeable and healthy (see chart on page 92), with pure air enriched by iodine and trace elements from the sea, lots of sunshine and temperatures which, in the evenings, drop to a pleasant level, conducive to a good night's sleep. A fresh breeze blows along the coast and is stronger in the south-west than on the sandy shores of the east. From May to October there is hardly any rainfall, although sometimes in the early morning there might be a little mist or low cloud. However, this will usually have cleared before midday. In the winter any showers which develop are usually followed by sunshine, while foggy days are almost unknown.

Moorish influence

There is a strong Arab influence throughout the Algarve, as it was here that the Moors ruled for the longest period of time. This is apparent in the white, cube-shaped, two-storeyed houses huddled together in the towns and villages, and in the lively Arabian fairy tales and sayings which are still so popular. Anything in the Algarve which happens to be very old, no matter whether it dates back to the Moorish period or not, is always referred to as *Coisas dos Mouros*. The beautifully decorated chimneys, which come in all shapes and sizes, and are so typical of the Algarve, were also introduced by the Moors, and some of them quite clearly resemble the minarets which adorn all Moorish mosques. Very often they are not actually chimneys at all, but used for ventilation control.

The people who live in the Algarve, generally known as Algarvios, combine temperament with serenity, unobtrusiveness with helpfulness and business sense with a cordial hospitality.

The rocky coast near Lagos

Specialities from the kitchen and wine cellar

There are many specialities in the Algarve which are not to be found in any other region of Portugal. From the Monchique Mountains comes the nourishing Medronho-Schnapps, very good for settling the stomach, as well as the light, sweet *Mel d'Oiro*, a kind of honey brandy containing Medronho. A fatty pork sausage is sometimes flambéd with Medronho and this dish is then known as *Chouriço com Medronho*. From the uplands comes a ham, which is dried in the open air and known as *Presunto*. A very popular Algarve dish, which the holidaymaker should certainly try, is *Ameijoas na Cataplana*, a delicious mixture of mussels, onions, tomatoes and ham, veal or sausage, cooked in a kind of pressure cooker.

Excursions

Another word on the range of excursions available in the Algarve. In addition to the holiday resorts mentioned here which offer tours by coach, car or boat, all the smaller towns provide coach tours with set itineraries. Most of these are day or half-day trips, but there are some which are longer, lasting in some cases for several days. Firms to note are Marcus and Harting of 69 Rua Conselheiro Bivar, Faro, and also of 2 Rua Caetano Fea, Praia da Rocha, as well as E.V.A., of Avenida da República, Faro.

The most popular outings are day trips to the Monchique Mountains with sightseeing in Silves, and a tour called 'Typical Algarve', which goes to Faro and to some of the most beautiful spots on the rugged coastline. The various outings and excursions to Lisbon are very much in demand and should always be booked well in advance.

The Rocky Coast of the Algarve

The Algarve coastline conjures up pictures of bizarre rock formations in

Ornamental chimney decoration in the Algarve

colours of red, yellow, brown or grey. These enclose sandy bays, both large and small, while other formations rise spectacularly out of the sea or create picturesque grottoes in the cliffs. This type of coastline dominates the western half of the Algarve, from Aljezur to Olhos de Agua near Albufeira. Most popular with tourists is the stretch between Sagres and Albufeira.

Owing to the increase in tourism and the amount of building which has taken place, much of the original atmosphere of the Algarve has, unfortunately, been lost. However, if you are prepared to make short trips on foot or by boat, you can still come across lovely bays in out-of-the-way places which are free from the madding crowd.

The best time for bathing, when the sea temperature is between 17° and 23°, is from the middle of May to the beginning of November. Other times of the year are fine for those who are

content to use a heated hotel swimming pool, take walks along lonely beaches, go fishing or play golf. There are plenty of opportunities for making contact with the local people and sampling the fare in small cafés, where fish is a speciality.

Sagres Alt. 40–62 m; Pop. 1,200 approx.

Sagres is the south-west tip of Europe, made famous by Henry the Navigator. Today it is a small but important fishing harbour with the largest lobster breeding grounds in Portugal. It is also a holiday centre for celebrities, anglers and gourmets, and is 116km from Faro, the airport which serves the Algarve.

The scenery can only be described as wild, almost Nordic in nature, with a bleak, windswept plateau and many cliffs between which the Atlantic breakers swirl and foam. For most of the time in the summer there is a very strong wind, but shelter can be found inside the little bays. On the other hand, from September to May there is hardly any wind at all.

The most interesting feature of Sagres is the rocky plateau, *Ponta de Sagres*, where a wonderful view can be obtained from the vantage point of the signal station. Here also is the *Fortaleza do Promontório*, Henry the Navigator's fortress, the gloomy walls of which encircle plain unadorned buildings. Here can be found the Chapel, *Santa Maria da Graça*, where there is a 15th c. stone compass. From the western bastion of the fort extends a magnificent view over the wild, steeply shelving coast as far as *Cape St Vincent*, at the foot of which a large craggy rock, the 'Giant', towers from the sea like a finger. For the Portuguese, the fortress at *Ponta de Sagres* is a national shrine. Prince Henry 'the Navigator', who was born in Oporto in 1394, has left his mark on Sagres. Here was created, under his direction, a School of Navigation which

Left: Camping in the Algarve

was the nerve centre, 'mission control' as it were, for the Portuguese contribution to world-wide exploration and discovery. Prince Henry died here in the year 1460, was buried in Lagos and his remains later taken to Batalha.

Sagres is not overrun by tourists. The rush of everyday life can soon be forgotten in this wild terrain and there is plenty of scope for relaxation.

Lying between the jutting cliffs of the plateau are several quiet, sandy beaches: *Baleeira*, with its fish quay and the hotel of the same name, is the largest in the town, *Martinhal*, offering a wide sandy bay with holiday bungalows, and *Mareta, Tonel* and *Beliche*, all surrounded by rock formations.

Fishing from the beach, underwater and deep-sea fishing are all available in the best stocked waters in Europe. Trips can be made with local fishermen, in boats holding 4 to 6 people, for 8,000 to 10,000 Escudos per day.

At the local Hotel *da Baleeira* and the *Orquidea* holiday apartments.

Good facilities, but your own equipment must be provided.

Especially turtle doves and hares.

About five establishments. Especially to be recommended is the fish restaurant *Tasca* in the Hotel da Baleeira. Sagres specialities include freshly caught lobsters, prepared in various ways, and *percebes* (polyp type barnacles with a rubbery skin rather than a firm shell) which live on the rocks in the tidal areas.

Colour films about Henry the Navigator and the Age of Discovery may be seen in the cinema at the Fortaleza do Promontório daily.

Cycles are on hire to hotel guests only at the Hotel da Baleeira.

If you do not go from Sagres to *Cape St Vincent* you will miss the highlight of your trip. From the balcony of the lighthouse, with the most powerful beam in Europe, you can see an ever-changing picture of waves breaking on the steeply shelving beaches and of large ships and small fishing boats moving across the vast expanse of the Atlantic. The cape is one of the few places in the world where you can watch the sun both rise and set over the sea. Close by the cape is the old fort, *Fort Beliche*, which has a very good restaurant.

15 km away on Route 125, near Rasposeira, stands an interesting Romanesque-Gothic chapel.

The same distance further on is the *Torre de Aspa* which, at 159m, is the highest rock on the west coast of the Algarve.

On the way to Lagos lies the little fishing village of *Salema*, 20 km away on the main road, but only 15 km if you go by bicycle on the side roads. There are a few bungalows and flats and it has a quiet beach.

Lagos Alt. 2-50 m; Pop. 17,000

Lying 78 km west of the airport at Faro, Lagos has more to offer than any other place in the Algarve, even in winter. It has a fishing harbour and is a centre for trade and industry (cork processing, marble, fish canning etc.), all of which provides added interest to the holiday. Its situation on a hill between a wide sandy bay and one of the most varied stretches of rocky coastline in the Algarve gives the widest possible choice to the holidaymaker. In Lagos everyone gets good value for money — the person looking for peace and quiet, the sportsman, the fun-lover, the gourmet and those interested in nature, art and history.

Like Sagres, Lagos is closely associated with Henry the Navigator and the Age of Discovery. Ships of new design were built here, including the caravels which, for the first time in the history of navigation, could sail against the wind. From here they set forth, the majority of them by way of Lisbon, on the greatest voyages of discovery the world has ever known. The Companhia de Lagos, founded in 1444, developed Portugal's trade links with Africa which had already begun with the opening of the first Portuguese slave market in Lagos in 1441.

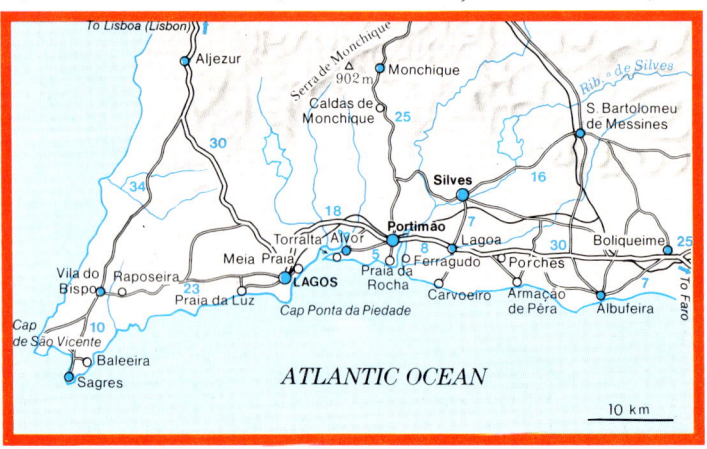

At the eastern end of Lagos is the sandy beach of *Meia Praia*, 5 km long. To the south and west, within a distance of 3 km and situated on the Golden Coast, are ten small bays, encompassed by the strange, shimmering, yellow rock formations which are a feature of the area. Among them are the beaches of *Dona Ana* and *Porto de Mós*.

Hotel *de Lagos*, Hotel *Golfinho*, Hotel *Meia Praia* (at the beach) and at the *Aquazul* apartment house.

From the beach and rocks. Equipment is available from the Luz Bay Sea Sports Centre in Praia de Luz, 3 km from Lagos.

In Porto de Mós and near the Dona Ana beach.

Arrangements can be made through the Hotel Meia Praia.

Sailing Club *de Velha* in Lagos harbour and the Hotel Golfinho.

From the Meia Praia beach.

From the Dona Ana beach.

From the beach and rocky coast. Night trips can be made on sardine fishing boats; enquiries should be made from your hotel porter or from the waiter of the Bar Barroca. Fishing is also available in the reservoir at *Bravura*, 15 km away.

Hares, partridges and doves.

At Palmares Golf Club, Meia Praia beach.

Hotel Meia Praia and Hotel de Lagos.

Hotel Golfinho.

Several inns of varying quality and popularity, mostly well established and with local atmosphere, such as the *Dom Sebastião* and the *Porta Velha*. Specialities include some excellent mussel dishes. Local wine from the wine cellars of Lagos is usually served.

Typical house of the Algarve

Several restaurants catering for international tastes.

In several hotels; also in discothèques *Machou* and *Phenix* and the *Jazz Club*.

Fado bar *A'Muralha*.

Hotel Meia Praia and in several other hotels.

In Praia da Luz on September 8th there is an important church festival with a procession of floats, folk dancing, team games, a fair, and fireworks in the evening; bullfights during the season.

Regional museum (containing archaeological finds and a collection of folk art items) near the Antonius Church; from the end of June to the end of August concerts take place in the larger churches.

Wrought iron work, copper ware and work in marble are all to be recommended.

Praça da República, the Square of the Republic, with the *Governor's Palace*; the *Old Customs House*, formerly the Slave Market; *Henry the Navigator's Palace*, which today is a hospital; and *Misericórdia* Church with its beautifully decorated and gilded wood-carved altar. *Igreja Santo António* is the finest Baroque church in the Algarve. Above a base laid with azulejos there are walls with gilded wood carvings, altars rich in gold and brightly painted ceilings. *Igreja São Sebastião*, with a magnificent Renaissance doorway and charnel house. On the hill there is the Square *Rossio da Trindade*, with attractive 18th c. houses and the remains of the old city wall.

Cycles can be hired in Lagos.

Go by bus, coach or on foot to the *Kap Ponta da Piedade* in order to see the most impressive, highly coloured and photogenic rock formations on the whole of the Algarve coast. Grottoes, natural arches of rock, rugged cliffs and crystal-clear pools of water abound, and it is situated only 2 km from the Dona Ana beach.

Praia da Luz

In the fishing village of Luz the white houses stretch from the rocks to the clear waters of a small bay. Situated only 5 km to the west of Lagos, the *Luz Bay Club* offers practically everything the holidaymaker could ask for.

To the cliffs of *Promontorio* about 1 km away.

Alvor and Torralta Alt. 5–30 m; Pop. 2,000

Half-way between Lagos and Praia da Rocha lies the small town of Alvor. Its long history is marked today only by a 16th c. parish church, *Igreja Matriz*, which was built on the site of a former mosque. In ancient times the town was a Greek port, after which it came under Moorish domination. During the Reconquest it became the burial place of King João III. Of special interest in the church, apart from the lovely font, are the heads of fishermen carved in stone, which act as capitals for the church columns, and the magnificent Manueline doorway.

Close by is the holiday centre of Torralta. Of all the holiday centres on the Algarve coast which are in the process of being developed, Torralta is the most advanced. Sandwiched in between the tall apartment blocks and the skyscraper hotels are the holiday bungalows and small apartment houses, at once reminding you of similar places on the Adriatic coast or on the Costa del Sol in Spain, but with very much more space on the sandy beaches.

The *Luxus* Hotel at *Alvor Praia*, where sand, sea and rocks meet, and the *Penina-Golf* Hotel, 3 km inland on the high ground of the Montes de Alvor, are both ideal places in which to relax.

Torralta lies close to the Arão estuary on the 9-km-long sandy bay of *Praia de Alvor* and *Meia Praia*. 4 km away, near *Praia da Rocha*, we come to the picturesque coast of *Praia dos Três Irmãos*.

Heated pools in Torralta at the Hotels *Alvor Praia, Delfim* and *Penina*.

Hotel Penina (4 km), 27 holes. International championships.

Hotel Alvor Praia.

Hotels Alvor Praia, Delfim and Penina, and in Torralta itself.

In Torralta.

Hotels Alvor Praia and Penina.

The sandy beach at Praia de Alvor is safe for children. All the hotels and apartment houses in Torralta welcome children.

⛶ ⊗ Hotels Alvor Praia and Delfim.

♪ Discothèque in Torralta.

♀ The Holiday Centre at Torralta. Nightclubs in the Hotels Alvor Praia and Penina.

⋈ ⚹ Casino, with a cabaret, adjacent to the Hotel Penina.

▲ In Alvor.

⚔ Bullfighting in Torralta during the season.

🚌 To Lagos and Praia da Rocha, both of which are about 5 km away. Coach tours. Beach walks, even at high tide.

Portimão Pop. 25,000

Portimão has the most important fishing harbour on the Algarve coast and is at the same time the urban hinterland of the seaside resort of Praia da Rocha, which is only 3 km away. The natural harbour was formed from the wide river estuary of the Rio Arade (Avo) and is used by a large number of fishing trawlers which mainly catch sardines.

At the fishmarket in Portimão there are regular auctions which are well worth going to see. A further attraction is the large cattle market which is held on the first Monday of every month.

⛶ Several excellent inns with typical Portuguese cuisine, of which the *Bicho* is particularly good for fish and shellfish of all sorts.

🛍 Jewellery, embroidery, porcelain, ceramics and woollen goods.

🚌 Just 2 km away, on the other side of the river and with a superb view, lies the still very traditional fishing village of *Ferragudo*. There are several typical inns which are used by the fishermen, a camping site and a discothèque. *Lagoa*, which is 7 km away, is interesting for its old-established wine cellars. The *Monchique Mountains* are only 18 km from Portimão.

Praia da Rocha Alt. 10–50 m; Pop. 1,000

The English were the first to spend their holidays in Praia da Rocha. This resort was really one of the pioneers, and today it is still a prime example of a successful international holiday resort in the Algarve. As a consequence, however, very little remains of the original atmosphere of this erstwhile peaceful little village.

Praia da Rocha, 67 km from the airport at Faro, is, for administrative purposes, included with the larger resort of Portimão, but it is, in fact, some 3 km distant, standing quite separate on a rocky plateau. The beach lies 10–50 m below and, like all the beaches on this rocky coast, is free from noisy streets and exhaust fumes.

The cliffs, rock formations and grottoes are especially varied and colourful. Many of the formations have been given names such as 'Triumphal Arch', 'Three Brothers' or 'Three Bears'. Because of its sheltered position, its facilities and its proximity to Portimão, Praia da Rocha has become a popular winter resort.

R The beach, which is full of small inlets, and the hinterland, which does not have many visitors, both offer plenty of scope for relaxation.

🛖 The rocky coast with its sandy bays stretches for about 3 km along both sides of the town. Adjacent to it, towards the west, is a 9-km-long beach. Eastwards a 2-km-long beach stretches as far as the Rio Arade, which is often called the Rio Avo or Ave.

⮕ Hotel *Algarve* with two heated pools. Hotel *Júpiter*.

🏄 🏊 S 🚣 ⚡

🎣 From the rocks, in the river (2 km away), from a boat or underwater with a snorkel.

Algarve: Rocky Coast

[Y] Hares and partridges.

[Q] *Aquazul* apartment house.

[/] Hotel *Penina*, near Alvor, 6 km away.

[♨] [Q] [SAUNA] Hotel Algarve.

[U] In Torralta, 4 km away.

[🏖] The beaches slope gently into the sea and are quite safe for children.

[✕] *Fortaleza* and several good restaurants in Portimão all specialising in local dishes. Try the grilled sardines or tuna fish from Portimão which are brought in daily. Local wine.

[♪] In the larger hotels.

[Y] About 6.

[🎸] In the Hotel Júpiter.

[✸] On August 1st and 2nd annually there is a church festival of *St Catherine* in Praia da Rocha, including a river procession and a beach Mass. On August 14th there is a fishing festival in Portimão.

[🛍] Good shops in the hotels. Large choice in Portimão.

[🚶] Along the cliff tops above the steeply shelving coastline or along the beach to Portimão (2–3 km).

[🚌] By bus to Portimão or to Lagos (about 10 km). Praia da Rocha is the nearest seaside resort to the *Monchique Mountains* (20–35 km).

Carvoeiro Alt. 5–70 m; Pop. 800

In the past few years this picturesque fishing village has greatly increased in size. In the thirties it was an exclusive resort, patronised by residents of Lisbon and by the British; now it has a wider

Praia da Rocha

range of visitors. Everything that could possibly be wanted on holiday is well provided for by this friendly little town, which is surrounded by cliffs. There are well furnished apartments and excellently appointed villas and bungalows on the cliff tops. Many people make excursions to Carvoeiro in order to see the dramatic rock and grotto formations at *Algar Seco* and the *Vale do Carvalho*.

[R] Ideal for romantics.

[⚓] Small sandy beach surrounded by cliffs and with fishing boats beached close to the main square.

[➚] Apartment house *Solférias*. Apartments *Quinta do Paraíso*, 1 km outside the town, and *Carvoeiro Clube*.

[🏊] [⚓] Ideal facilities near the cliffs on each side of the town.

	Apartment house Solférias and Quinta do Paraíso apartments.

	Boite and *Sobe e Desce*.

	Hotel *Dom Sancho*.

	The Festival of *Senhora da Incarnação* takes place on the last Sunday in August.

	On foot, by boat or by car eastwards to the beauty spots of *Algar Seco* and *Carvalho*. 6 km away is Lagoa with its famous wine cellars.

Armação de Pêra Alt. 4–15 m; Pop. 2,000

From being a picturesque and lively little fishing village, Armação de Pêra has developed into a most popular resort. Stretching out to the east are the sand dunes, while westwards the cliffs, broken up by small bays and grottoes, reach as far as the Avo estuary near Portimão.

	Lonely walks along footpaths on the cliff tops, in the bays and among the sand dunes.

	Fine, white sandy beaches well protected from the wind abound in the bays. In addition there is a 4-km-long stretch of beach with sand dunes, sloping very gently into the sea.

	Hotel *do Garbe*, Hotel *Levante* and Hotel *Viking* which is 3 km from the town.

		Hotel Viking.

	From the rocks, from a boat or underwater.

	Hotel *Vilalara*, 2 km from the town, and Hotel *Nelson*.

		Hotel Viking.

🅰 2 km from the town.

🛏 Close by the Hotel do Garbe.

🔑 By arrangement with the *Casa Agricular Sol e Mar*.

🏖 The sea is calm for most of the time, and the beach with the sand dunes is the most suitable for children. In fact, the beach is called *Praia das Crianças* (the children's beach). There are also children's swimming baths at the Hotel Viking and Hotel Levante.

🍴 🍽 Grills are a speciality at the *Panorama* restaurant.

🎵 🍷

🎭 The Festival of the Fishermen takes place in August. On the third Sunday in September there is a church festival, *Nossa Senhora dos Aflitos*.

🚶 Along the beach or along the cliffs to the cliff-top chapel of *Nossa Senhora dos Aflitos*, parts of which are Romanesque.

🚌 Trips by boat to the grottoes or to Carvoeira, for which arrangements should be made through the tourist office. To *Porches*, 5 km away, with its large workshops making hand-painted ceramics.

Albufeira Alt. 20–180 m; Pop. 15,000

Albufeira is an ancient town. The Romans called it Baltum and the Moors, who occupied it from the 8th to the middle of the 13th centuries, named it Al-Buhar. The picture of the town today is still one of closely grouped white houses, Moorish in style, but earthquake, flood and finally a great fire in 1893 destroyed almost the whole of the old town. Albufeira is situated just 36 km from Faro airport and is one of the more popular resorts on the Algarve coast, even in winter. The town, sited on the cliff top, spreads out over the neighbouring slopes, enclosing the main beach and the fish quay like an amphitheatre.

ℹ️ Despite the activity in the market and the crowds of holidaymakers, those who wish to relax can still find plenty of opportunities to do so in and around the town.

🏖 Although very rocky, sandy bays can still be found towards the east; westwards the coast is much wilder.

🏊 Hotels *Boavista* (heated), *Sol e Mar* (covered), *Alfa Mar* (two swimming pools) and *Albufeira Jardim*.

🎣 Among the rocks.

🏃 ⚡

👶 Alfa Mar hotel

💆 Adjacent to the Sol e Mar Hotel.

🎾 *Aldeira Turistica de S. João* (3 km) and Hotel Albufeira Jardim.

SAUNA Hotel Albufeira Jardim.

🐴 Donkey rides and a children's playground at the *Rancho da Orada* 2 km to the west.

🅰 On the edge of the town.

🍴 There are a large number of restaurants varying in popularity and offering local speciality dishes, many of which have become rather expensive. Among the better ones are *Ruina*, on the fish market; *António* (3 km, on the way to Guia) and *Borda d'Agua* (3 km east on the Praia da Ouro, 'the Golden Beach'). Apart from these, there are several fish restaurants all of which give good value.

🍽 Highly commended by connoisseurs is the cuisine of the *Casa da Torte* 3 km to the east, and the *Castelo*, on the beach of the same name, is also very popular.

🎵 5 or 6 discothèques and dance halls.

🍸 Several in the town and in the hotels.

☕ *Café Bailote* with an exhibition of Cubist art and paintings by the fisherman and café proprietor João Barreto Bailote.

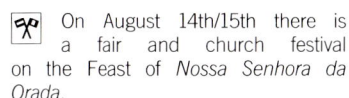

✂ On August 14th/15th there is a fair and church festival on the Feast of *Nossa Senhora da Orada*.

On September 3rd there is a church festival on the Feast of *Beato Vincente*.

Bullfights take place during the season.

🎸 Once weekly at the *International Club*.

🚶 On the beach at low tide and along the cliffs.

🚌 5 km eastwards across the *Maria Luisa* beach to the *Club Méditerranée Balaia* where there is a heated swimming pool, a night club and a mini-golf course. There are also some tennis courts.

8 km further on to the east lies the holiday resort of *Olhos de Agua* which is almost exclusively frequented by the Portuguese themselves. At low water, clear drinking water gushes from freshwater springs under the sea. In the grounds of the *Alfa Mar* Hotel and the *Montechoro* luxury hotel and bungalow complex there are facilities for tennis and swimming, as well as a sauna and a restaurant.

The Sandy Coast of the Algarve

The almost rock-free sandy coastline of the Algarve begins about 8 km to the east of Albufeira and stretches beyond Faro as far as the Spanish border near Vila Real de Santo António. Here the cliffs and rock formations are replaced by sand dunes and sandy beaches which slope gently into the sea.

Albufeira

Between Anção to the west of Faro and Cacela to the east of Tavira small lagoons and pools of seawater have been formed between the dunes and the seashore. The easterly part of the Algarve coast is particularly suitable for visitors looking for smooth sandy beaches and a warm climate, but who also require something different from the Italian Adriatic coast. This part of the Algarve is ideal for families with small children. The average air temperatures here are some 2° to 3° higher than in the rocky parts of the Algarve, and the water temperature is about 1° higher.

Praia de Falésia

The well appointed holiday village of *Aldeia dos Açoteias* is about 12 km from Vilamoura. The majority of the holiday villas and bungalows are built in the typical Portuguese fashion, with balconies and open fireplaces.

🏖 A sandy beach to which there is a free bus service is 2 km away.

🚶

⚡ **S** In Vilamoura.

🛶 The beach is quite safe for children. There is a children's swimming pool and baby-sitting facilities are available.

In the holiday village or in the nearby *Alfa Mar* Hotel.

In the holiday village.

At the Alfa Mar Hotel.

Vilamoura and Quartiera Alt. 5–20 m; Pop. 2,000

Stretches of vast, long, sandy beaches are broken here and there by bays and estuaries. Vilamoura is the centre of a huge development, covering an area of about 300 sq. km, which has been taking place over the last few years, and it is clear that construction work will be going on for many years to come.

Vilamoura

An extensive modern holiday centre is being developed here. Only phase 1, which includes holiday homes, apartments, restaurants, a swimming pool, two 18-hole golf courses and a tennis court, has so far been completed. At the splendid Marina, which has been extended and is now one of the largest on the whole of the Algarve coast, there is a big shopping complex.

Estalagem da Cegonia, 9 km away, is an equestrian centre which has an indoor riding school and its own guest house. The large beach, which is usually very crowded, is about 3 km from the holiday centre in Vilamoura. On the beach itself, there is an apartment block and three large hotels. As the holiday complex here is so vast a car is really necessary.

The extensive woodland and forest which surround Vilamoura offer the best opportunities for relaxation.

Very long, wide beach.

Hotels Dom Pedro, Atlantis and Vilamoura Marinhotel.

Hotels Dom Pedro, Atlantis and Vilamoura Marinhotel.

Baby-sitting can be arranged during the season.

Casino with cabaret.

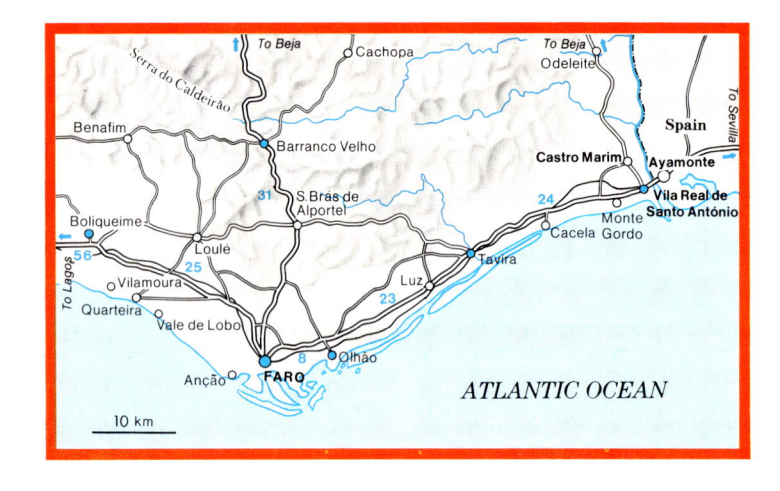

Algarve: Sandy Coast 47

[icon] Motorboat trips along the coast may be arranged at the hotels or at the Marina.

Quartiera

About 5 km east of Vilamoura is Quartiera, previously a rather insignificant little town but now developing into quite a successful holiday resort. There has been considerable building along the seafront but, unlike Vilamoura's, the town centre has survived. There are a few old original bars and restaurants with a typically Portuguese atmosphere.

[icon] A not particularly wide beach with new breakwaters.

[icon] Hotel *Quartiera Sol* and Hotel *Dom José*.

[icons]

[icon] Hotel Quartiera Sol.

[icons]

[icon] Bullfights take place during the season. On December 8th the feast of *Feira Nossa Senhora Conceicão* is celebrated with a religious procession.

Vale de Lobo

About 4 km to the east of Quartiera, on the way to Faro, you come to *Vale de Lobo*, the Valley of the Wolf, which is surrounded by a vast pine forest. Here, where the sandy beaches are broken by small outcrops of rock, there has grown up one of the most beautiful holiday centres in the Algarve. The luxurious hotel *Dona Filipa* and a number of villas and bungalows are set among the woodlands and lawns.

[icon] Long stretches of sandy beach; small but very peaceful bays a little way from the resort.

[icon] Two swimming pools, one of which is heated. Some of the holiday homes have their own pools.

[icon] The wide smooth beach is partially enclosed and has a lifeguard in attendance. There is a small tennis court for the use of children, a children's swimming pool and a very well equipped play area. Baby-sitting can be arranged.

[icons]

[icon] The largest complex of tennis courts in the Algarve. Coaching is available.

[icon] 18- and 27-hole golf courses at *Quinta do Lago*. Golf lessons available.

SAUNA

[icons]

[icon] Once a week.

[icon] Through the pine forests. Bicycles may be hired.

Faro Pop. 20,000

Faro, the provincial capital and commercial centre of the Algarve, has the only airport in southern Portugal. Although Faro has no really outstanding sights, it is an ideal shopping centre and is well worth a visit for that reason alone. If you like beaches which are hot and sunny and you wish to mix freely with the local people, then Faro, with its long sweep of sand dunes behind the seawater lagoons, would be a very suitable place for a holiday.

History. As long ago as the 4th c. Faro was a cathedral city, but it came under Moorish rule from the 8th c. until 1249, when the Moors were finally driven out of Portugal following the Battle of Faro.

Francisco Gomes completely rebuilt the city in the 18th c., after it had been devastated by two earthquakes. The best view over Faro and the coast can be obtained from the observation tower near the Chapel of *Santo António do Alto*, on the south-eastern edge of the town. In the chapel, which is situated on the site of an old Greek shrine, is the small *António* ecclesiastical museum containing a priceless 12th c. painting of Saint Anthony by the Italian artist Giotto (opening times: 9 a.m.–1 p.m. and 2 p.m.–sunset).

Sights of Faro. The main attractions are all to be found on the waterfront; a good place to start from is at the harbour on the *Praça de Dom Francisco Gomes*, where there are a large number of palm trees and several very charming cafés.

From there you can go to the Port Authority building, which houses the *Navigation and Fishing Museum* (opening times: Mon.–Fri. 9.30 a.m. to 12.30 p.m. and 2–5.30 p.m., Sat. 9 a.m.–1 p.m., closed Sundays). By walking through the gardens of the *Jardim Manuel Bivar*, you come to one of the gateways in the old part of the city, the *Arco da Vila*.

On the *Largo da Sé* stands the cathedral, dating back originally to the 13th c., but which was rebuilt following the earthquake of 1755. Of the original building only the tower and the main doorway remain, but the ceramic tiles, mostly from the 17th c., are still intact. Behind the cathedral is the former 16th c. convent, *Nossa Senhora da Assunção*, which has a splendid Gothic doorway, two-storey cloisters and the *Archaeological Museum* (opening times: Tues.–Sun. 10 a.m.–noon and 2–5 p.m.; closed Mon.). The greatest attraction in the museum is a Roman floor mosaic which is approximately 2,000 years old.

Not far from the cathedral stands one of the most interesting churches in the city. Inside the twin-towered Baroque *Igreja Nossa Senhora do Carmo* there are 18th c. carvings and the 19th c. Chapel *des Ossos*, an ossuary chapel, the walls of which are decorated with skulls and bones.

At the end of the extensive pedestrian zone stands the new *Regional Ethnographical Museum* (opening times: Mon.–Fri. 10 a.m.–12.30 p.m. and 2–6 p.m., Sat. 10 a.m.–1 p.m., closed Sun.). In addition to a display of costumes, furniture, and tools used in the fishing industry, there is also a model of a typical village street in the Algarve.

7 km by car in the direction of the airport, or by boat from Porta Nova which involves a journey over the mud flats, there is a long, narrow, sandy beach between the lagoons and the sand dunes.

At the Hotel *Eva*.

Several choices available.

Processions during Holy Week. The festival of *Feira do Carmo* takes place annually from July 15th to 30th. In August there is the City of Faro Festival and at the end of October the Feast of *Santa Iria*, which includes a fair.

The Rua Santo António and its side streets are good places for shopping expeditions. Confectionery, made of figs with almonds, embroidery, painted tiles or ceramics, wines and spirits, copper ware, raffia and wicker work all make good gifts to take home.

By car or coach to *Olhão* (8 km) and to *São Brás de Alportel* (19 km) where, on a delightful ridge among olive, orange and almond trees, stands a pousada (government-sponsored inn), the view from which is considered to be

Right: Faro

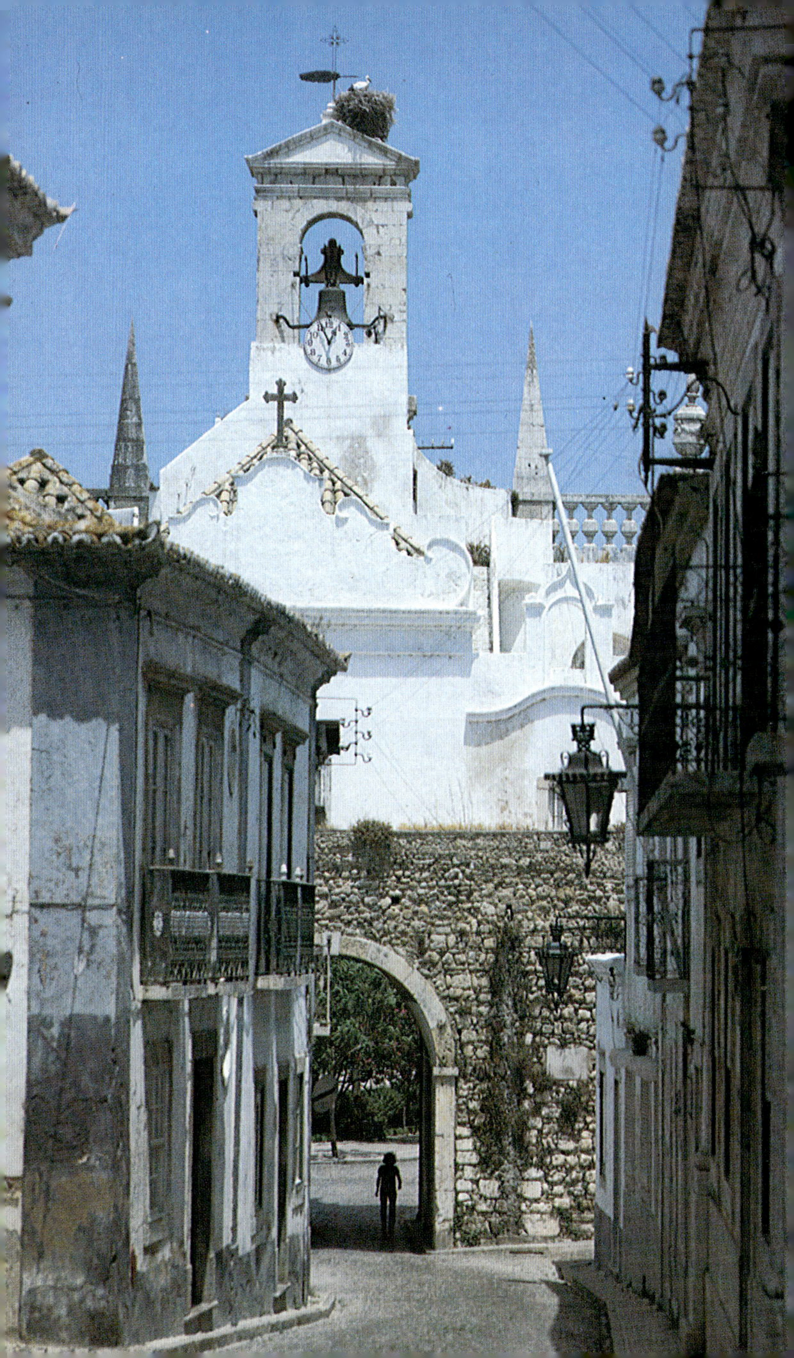

one of the finest in the Algarve. On the way to São Brás you pass through the town of *Estoi*, where there is an 18th c. castle with a symetrically laid out park which is worth a visit. Not quite so interesting, although probably more well known, are the ruins of *Milreu*, which are 1,400 years old.

Olhão Pop. 12,000

Olhão is North Africa in Portugal. The port, 8 km east of Faro, was constructed in the 18th c. in a typical Arab style of architecture as a result of Portugal's trading links with Africa. The white, cube-shaped houses are tightly packed together and it is worth just climbing on to one of the flat roofs in order to see how the cubes are placed, one virtually on top of the next, a practice known as 'mirantes' and 'contramirantes'. The houses are linked together by outside steps.

Olhão, however, is not only interesting because of its unusual architecture. This small port has been, for many years, the principal harbour on the whole Portuguese coast for the fishing of tuna. It is no surprise, therefore, that the waterfront is of more interest than the rest of the town. Don't miss a visit to the harbour even if the smell from the fish-processing plant is enough to put you off!

Near the harbour, on the *Praça da Restauração*, stands the parish church of *Nossa Senhora do Rosario*, which was built in the 17th c. by local fishermen. The close connection of the town with the tuna fishing industry is shown on many tiles with motifs depicting the lives of the fishermen. Very fine examples of these tiles are to be found on the *Domus Justicia* building.

There are regular ferry connections with the *Cabo Santa Maria*. If you wish to go swimming, you should go by boat to the island beach of *Armona*.

Tavira Alt. 5–50 m; Pop. 12,000

Tavira is a very old town situated close to the mouth of the Rio Séqua, half-way between Faro and the Spanish border. Its origins go back to Greek settlements but later the city came under Roman rule. The most visible sign of the Roman occupation is the foundations of a seven-arched bridge which still remain today. At a later date it became an important military base for the Moors, and later still, the seat of residence of several Portuguese kings. Very little now remains of the resplendent past of this city, which earned for itself the name of 'Algarvian Rome'. Its 36 churches were almost completely destroyed in the earthquake of 1755. The ruins of the Moorish *castle*, however, are still very impressive and provide a good view over the city from its ramparts. Close by is the Church of *Santa Maria*, which has a well preserved Gothic doorway, and inside which are the most beautiful tiles dating back to the 17th and 18th centuries.

Further on is the *Misericórdia* with a lovely Renaissance doorway. Inside, the church has some very ornate pillars gilded in the Rococo style and a beautifully carved altar. In the same area, there are many interesting small churches and typical little Algarve houses with richly decorated chimneys.

A special tip

In July and August the Tourada marítima takes place. At that time immense shoals of tuna swim past the coast, and the spectacle of the Portuguese fishermen hauling in their huge catches, although fascinating to watch, is also a somewhat gory one. Although a fisherman will rarely take a tourist to the Tourada with him, it is still worth making the effort to watch the nets being hauled in, if only to capture the atmosphere which pervades this small romantic town.

Typical Algarve hillside town

There is a sandy beach on *Tavira Island* which can be reached by boat and/or coach. There are also beaches at *Cabanas* and *Barril*.

Eurohotel, *Quinta das Oliveiras* and the holiday complexes *Pedras da Rainha*, 6 km outside the town, and *Pedras del Rei*, which is 5 km away.

At the Hotel Quinta das Oliveiras.

At the Hotel Quinta das Oliveiras as well as at Pedras da Rainha and Pedras del Rei.

Pedras da Rainha and Pedras del Rei.

On New Year's Day there is a folk music competition called *Concurso de Charolas*.

Outing to the little fishing village of *Santa Luzia*, 3 km away, which is still very traditional and has an extensive beach.

Monte Gordo 5–15 m; Pop. 1,000.
Monte Gordo, near Vila Real de San António, is one of the better known resorts on this stretch of the Algarve coast. It combines the natural beauty of the pine forests, beaches and sand dunes with the more sophisticated character of a spa town, and it provides many opportunities for a most enjoyable holiday.

On the beach and in the vast pine forests.

Long sandy beaches sloping gently into the sea.

At the Hotels *Vasco da Gama*, *Alcazar*, and *Navegadores*.

In the estuary.

Hotel Navegadores.

Hotel *Vasco da Gama*.

In the Carapeto part of the town, but only with untrained horses.

Ideal beach for children. There is a children's playground at the Hotel

Algarve: Sandy Coast

Vasco da Gama. Baby-sitting is available at the majority of the hotels.

△ Superb camping site, including a tennis court, in a terraced pine grove between Monte Gordo and Vila Real.

✕ *Dom Jotta*, at the mouth of the Guadiana river, and typical fish restaurants in Vila Real.

✕ In the hotels.

♪ Several discothèques; there is also a band at the Hotel Vasco da Gama.

♀ ✕ Several bars and a casino; there is a night-club at the Hotel Vasco da Gama.

✂ On May 13th there is a candlelit procession and in mid August a procession and a fair. On the second Sunday in September, the feast of *Nossa Senhora dos Dores*, there is a procession. A carnival takes place in Vila Real.

⇥ In Vila Real.

🚶 Along the beach or west through the sand dunes and pine forests for about 4 km as far as *Praia Verde*. A longer walk would be to *Cacela*, about 9 km. Along a woodland path for 4 km to Vila Real and then along the bank of the river for a further 4 km to *Castro Marim* Castle (see Vila Real).

🚌 To *Vila Real* (4 km, also by horse-drawn cab) and from there to *Castro Marim* or by ferry to the Spanish border town of *Ayamonte*.

Vila Real de Santo António Alt. 5–15 m; Pop. 12,000

4 km from the mouth of the Rio Guadiana, which marks the frontier between Portugal and Spain, and situated on the banks of that river, lies the little port of Vila Real. It has rather a distinctive smell about it as it has developed into a centre of the fish processing industry.

From the town's main square, *Praça Marquês de Pombal*, which is laid out with black pavement mosaics and which has a statue of King José I, you soon come to a lovely riverside walk and to the fish quays where a daily market is held. A large covered meat and vegetable market is situated close to the pedestrian zone. This town is not well equipped for those tourists thinking of spending some time here: apart from a few small pensions there is practically nowhere for an overnight stay.

✕ 🍲

☂ Temporary exhibitions in the *Galeria Municipal*.

✂ Carnival and Battle of Flowers; bullfights in June, July and August.

🚌 To the Spanish frontier town of *Ayamonte*; connections by car ferry from Vila Real, in the main tourist season until midnight, otherwise until about 8 p.m. To the seaside resort of *Monte Gordo* (4 km). To *Castro Marim*; this town is situated on a hill about 4 km from Vila Real in the middle of an extensive salt-marsh.

The whole of the countryside around Castro Marim is given over to a nature reserve where 23 different species of sea birds spend the winter months. The town itself is dominated by the ruins of the former knights of Christ Castle which was built in 1336 by the Knights of the military Order of Gil Marim. The first castle to belong to the Order of the Knights of Christ was in Tomar. On a hill opposite stand the ruins of Fort *São Sebastião*. In Castro Marim is an interesting chapel dedicated to *Nossa Senhora dos Mártires*.

Boat trips on the River Guadiana are sometimes arranged; these are to be recommended, as the river flows through some very attractive country. Information may be obtained from the Tourist Information Office in Vila Real.

Almond blossom in the Algarve

The Garden-countryside of the Algarve

Sandwiched between the foothills of the mountains and the coast is a 10–20-km-wide stretch of delightful fertile countryside, a veritable fruit and vegetable garden. Apart from the favourable climate and the rich soil, another factor contributing to its horticultural prosperity is the irrigation system, part of which goes back to the time of the Arab occupation. In this 'Garden of Eden' millions of almond trees — which come into blossom at the end of January — oranges, lemons, figs, tomatoes, asparagus, strawberries and many other kinds of fruit flourish. Wine is produced almost everywhere but especially in the countryside around Lagoa. Rice is grown in the area between Portimão and Lagos. The gardens are in full bloom from February to November, making striking contrasts between the whites of the houses and the reds of the roses and geraniums.

Lagoa Pop. 5,700

If, starting out from the eastern part of the Algarve coast, you want to visit Praia da Rocha, Lagos or Sagres or, conversely, you travel from one of those

Drying figs in the sun

places to Albufeira and Faro, you will without doubt pass through Lagoa. Tourists are always pleased to stay in this impressive little town as it is the province's chief wine producer. Wine, chiefly red, may be sampled in, or purchased from, the wine cellars. In particular there is a choice sherry which is stored in old oak casks for at least five years.

Silves Pop. 11,000

In the golden age of Moorish rule in Portugal, Silves, the centre of the Algarve, was more influential and prosperous than Lisbon itself. The Moorish castle which dominates the landscape was almost destroyed in the course of time but has been carefully restored. However, the cathedral, which lies immediately next to the castle, is historically more important. Built on the site of an old mosque, it is in the Gothic style, but with elements reminiscent of the Romanesque period, and has a large Manueline window facing its splendid doorway.

Loulé Alt. 170–200 m; Pop. 17,000

Just like Silves, Loulé dates back to Moorish times, but very little remains to remind us of that period. There are, however, many lovely Algarvian chimneys to be seen.

Loulé is very popular among Algarve holidaymakers as a good shopping centre. In the market hall, not only are provisions and flowers for sale, but there are also lovely baskets and pottery. Copper products may be purchased here which are cheaper than in most other Algarve towns. Confectionery makes a very popular present and you can get many different specialities in Loulé.

The Loulé Carnival lasts for three days, ending in a spectacular battle of flowers. Every year in April the pilgrimage to *Nossa Senhora da Piedade* takes place, and is regarded as the greatest church festival in the Algarve. There is plenty of scope for the photographer wishing to capture on film some of the many examples of local tradition.

It is worth taking a trip from Loulé to *Almansil*, some 5 km to the east. The whole interior of its Baroque church, including the ceiling, is covered with beautiful blue azulejos. The houses in this tiny township are distinguished by their chimneys of various shapes.

The Mountain Region of the Algarve

A 400–900-m-high chain of mountains, some 155 km long, forms the hinterland of the Algarve, but at no point is it further than 50 km from the coast. The Monchique Mountains, which lie north of the rocky coast area, are by far the most important and beautiful part of the mountain range. Pines, mimosas, strawberry trees (arbutus), sweet chestnuts and walnuts are just some of the trees which grow here. Cork oaks are abundant in the area and every nine years, when their bark is removed, they almost appear to glow as the reddish-brown chocolate colour of their naked trunks is so rich. Cork is one of Portugal's most important exports.

Medronho Schnapps is distilled from the fruit of a particular variety of the strawberry tree which, like many other flowering plants, is almost unique to the area of the Monchique Mountains. Among the woodlands there are also rocky gorges, waterfalls, grassy glades and trout streams.

Silves

Silves

Monchique Alt. 455–600m; Pop. 10,000

Monchique is in the middle of the mountain range of the same name and is the usual point of departure for a climb to the peak of the 902-m-high Foia. From here too there is an enjoyable mountain walk to the vehicle-free town of Picota, which stands at 774 m, and is the best place to buy Medronho Schnapps as well as walnuts and air-dried ham (a tip: eat them both together).

It is a dream place for romantics and it would be well worth the while of any visitor to the coast to spend at least one day of the holiday in Monchique. Here you could spend time among the gorges, waterfalls and woodland paths of the area, or visit the semi-wild 'spa park' of Caldas de Monchique or the nearby ruins of a 17th c. Franciscan convent. Half-way up the mountain, from the Estalagem *Abrigo da Montanha*, an outstanding panoramic view of the Foia can be obtained, its moods and colours changing dramatically from morning to evening. You may picnic here under the trees, but if you wish to stay, prior booking is advisable.

São Brás de Alportel Pop. 7,650

This mountain resort on the southern foothills of the *Serra do Caldeirão*, which lie 19 km north of Faro, provides a natural vantage point over the garden-country and coastal region of the Algarve. In early spring, the town's government-sponsored pousada (book early!) is an ideal base for walks through the enormous almond orchards, covered by a sea of blossom, and along the orange groves, the trees of which bear fruit and blossoms at the same time. It is 25 km from São Brás on Highway N2 to the *Belvedere do Caldeirão* (544 m), the most splendid vantage point in the Serra.

From the Tagus to the Algarve

The countryside between and adjoining the coastal provinces of Estremadura and the Algarve is hardly ever visited by those tourists arriving in Portugal by air, while those travelling by car usually drive straight through. This is a pity, because there are a number of quaint old towns which are well worth seeing, tucked away in the fascinating, ever-changing scenery. Hillsides with their forests of cork-oak, olive plantations and beautiful river valleys alternate with vast cornfields, orange groves and orchards. The roads are often bordered with hedges of gorse, mimosa and eucalyptus which sometimes stretch for miles. The lack of natural lakes is made up for by the number of large dams which have been constructed in the area.

Marvão Alt. 862 m; Pop. 300 approx.

Marvão is an old sleepy fortress town, positioned on a steep mountain top in the *Serra de São Mamede*, close to the Spanish border and 15 km to the west of a mountain pass leading to Madrid. The plateau is dominated by a large castle, the perfectly preserved walls of which enclose not only the castle grounds but also the small town itself. Some of the houses have already become vacant as the young people move away in order to find employment. The visitor, however, enjoys a wonderful panoramic view over the mountains, forests and fertile plains with their little towns and villages scattered around. The best time to enjoy this sight is in the morning or late afternoon, when it is at its most atmospheric. Accommodation may be found in the well run pousada, but prior booking is essential.

Castelo de Vide Alt. 460 m; Pop. 4,000

It is almost as if time had been standing still here since the Middle Ages. Castelo de Vide is one of the most picturesque and friendly towns in Portugal. White houses, with steps leading from one to another, many fountains, masses of flowers — and all overlooked by a half-ruined 12th c. castle. If you can manage to climb the very steep alleyways to get up there, you will have a superb view over the town from this spot.

Portalegre Pop. 14,000

This town, 20 km to the south of Marvão, is notable for its Baroque churches and palaces which include the cathedral, the *Bonfim* and the *Misericórdia* churches, the Town Hall and the *Amerelo Palace*. The *São Bernardo* Monastery and the *Melo Palace* both date back to the 16th c., but even older is the *Santa Clara* Convent which was built in the 14th c. Visits to the District Museum and to the Museum of Church Art are worth while. There is a lovely view from the top of the 13th c. *Atalaião* tower. The town is famous for its manufacture of tapestries.

Elvas Pop. 17,000

Elvas, 12 km west of the frontier pass leading to the Spanish town of Badajoz, is such a charming town that it is sometimes a little overrated. It cannot, for instance, be compared with Évora. Places of interest, however, include the *Largo Santa Clara*, with a Moorish gate and a remarkable stone column, the small but splendid monastery chapel of *São Domingos* and the cathedral. This rather massive-looking building will surprise you once you are inside, with its finely painted ceilings and beautiful azulejos. For the tourist, however, that part of the town close to the fortifications does not offer a great deal of interest.

From the N4 National Highway you can get a good view of the enormous 15th to 16th c. aqueduct which, in places, is four storeys high.

Vila Viçosa Pop. 5,000

If you take the Évora-Estremoz-Elvas road (or the opposite direction) do not miss a visit to the former seat of the Bragança dynasty. This Renaissance palace, built of locally quarried marble, stands alongside the large square, the *Terreiro do Paço*, and has beautiful public gardens. On the other side of the square is the Augustinian church, which is not of any great interest, but do not overlook the unique 'Bone Gate' *(Porta dos Nós)* when you leave the town heading north.

Estremoz Alt. 400–500 m; Pop. 12,000

Don't miss seeing Estremoz just because it has now been bypassed. The lower town is particularly worth visiting on a Saturday when the weekly market is held on the large *Rossio Square*. The red pottery so typical of Estremoz can be found among the many other things which are for sale. The picturesque, Moorish upper town is built around the imposing 13th c. castle, part of which has been converted into an elegant pousada. There is a spectacular view from the crenellated watch-tower. The Church of *Santa Maria do Castelo*, which is of the Manueline and Renaissance periods, stands on the Castle Square.

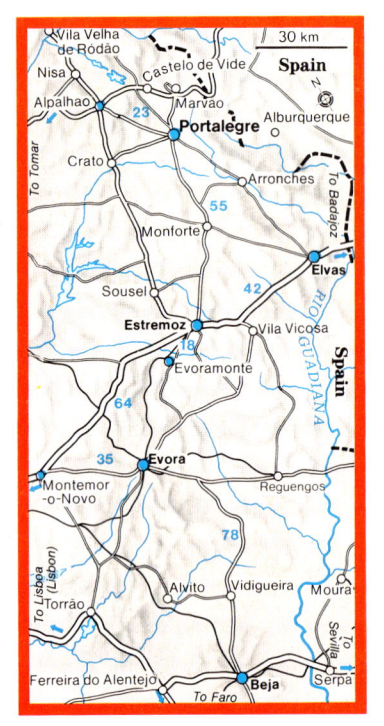

Évoramonte Pop. 2,000

Lying 18 km to the south-west of Estremoz, and situated on the top of a high hill from where there is a perfect all-round view, is the small fortified town of Évoramonte. Its clean alleyways and small white houses, all decorated with flowers, radiate peace and tranquillity. The castle dating from the 14th to the 16th c. is also worth visiting.

Évora Alt. 250–300 m; Pop. 40,000

Évora, one of the oldest towns on the Iberian peninsula, is widely considered to be the finest small provincial town in Portugal and is often referred to as the 'museum town'. Even as far back as Roman times, Évora (Ebora) was the capital of the province of Lusitania, and it was a cathedral town under the West Goths. The Moors were in occupation from the beginning of the 8th c. to A.D. 1160, and from 1200 onwards it was the seat of residence of Portuguese kings of the Burgundian and Aviz dynasties. From the 14th to the 16th c. it ranked as the second largest town in Portugal and was a cultural centre. From 1551 to 1759 it was a university town and, following a period of relative insignificance, it has now become an important tourist centre.

When it is referred to as the museum town, it is not because of Évora's museums, of which it has very few, but because of the evidence from the past which collectively represents an unrivalled and unique museum in itself.

Évora

There is always the danger, when trying to take in all the sights, that something might be left out, and a tried and tested round trip, which takes about four hours on foot, including time for sightseeing, is highly recommended. This trip can be extended by taking short walks along many of the interesting side streets.

The best place to start from is the large square called *Praça do Giraldo*, with its lovely arches, fountains from the Renaissance period and the Church of *Santo Antão* of the same period. Go down the *Rua de 5 de Outubro* and come to the Gothic cathedral with its lingering Romanesque influence. Once inside it is worth going up from the central aisle to the high chancel with its splendid Renaissance choir stalls. Just a little higher up is the roof terrace.

To the left of the cathedral can be seen the Regional Museum and 14 pillars of the Roman Temple of Diana, dating back to the 2nd or 3rd century. Part of the predominantly Manueline *Palácio Cadaval*, including the cloisters, has been converted into one of the best pousadas in the country. Turn left outside the palace and you come to the former seat of the Order of the Knights of Christ, now the *Paça dos Condes de Basto*, parts of which date back to the time of the West Goths. The old university is an immense Renaissance building, incorporating many examples of the Baroque style, and is situated close by. Don't miss the church and inner courtyard. From here you go straight back to the cathedral, behind which you turn left to the Moorish Gate on the *Largo das Portas de Moura*, with its beautiful fountains, and the *Casa Cordovil*, a mansion in the Moorish style. Here, for a small tip, you can climb on to the roof terrace and, framed by Moorish arches, have your photograph taken against one of the most superb backdrops in Évora.

Now, back to the Moorish Gate and turn left to the *Misericórdia* Church, with its Baroque carved altar, and a little further on, the Renaissance *Graça* Church. Nearby is the *Real de São Francisco* Church, an important Gothic-Manueline building, which has a macabre ossuary chapel, the ceiling and walls of which are covered with human bones. From here you should go, still heading towards the town wall, to the *Galeria das Damas* and the Arabic-Gothic style *Palácio Dom Manuel*, which is set in a lovely park. Via the monastery chapel of Santa Clara (Baroque with Renaissance cloisters and gilded carving) the walk takes you back to Giraldo Square.

Beja Pop. 18,000

Beja is the most important point of intersection for north-south/east-west traffic in southern Portugal. For many the main attraction is the watch-tower, built in 1310, with its views for miles around; it is Portugal's highest castle tower. On a visit to Beja go past the *Misericórdia* Church (Renaissance) to the *Largo do Povir* and have a quick look at the Church of *Santa Maria* with its Gothic doorway and Baroque interior. You can now spend a good hour viewing the former convent, *Nossa Senhora da Conceição*, which is one of the earliest examples of the Manueline style. Today it is a Regional Museum, containing a large variety of antiquities, coats-of-arms, weapons, costumes, paintings, azulejos etc.

Moura Pop. 10,000

When you leave Beja it is worth while taking a trip to the small fortified town of Moura. The Gothic church of *São João Baptista* has a Manueline doorway and is rich in azulejo decoration. In addition to the other churches and monasteries, the *Tres Bicas* fountain and the *Mouraria*, the old Moorish quarter, are particularly noteworthy.

Portugal's little known North

'Take it easy in Lisbon, work in Oporto' is a Portuguese saying which perfectly characterises the difference between the wealthy south, prosperous on account of its trade, industry and tourism, and the north of the country which has lagged behind. Even today the tourist industry regards north Portugal as an unloved, neglected child and looks upon this region as scarcely more than an extension of the sunny Algarve coast. Consequently the visitor may miss out on many things of interest. The delightful old town of Oporto, the centre of the north, compares favourably with Lisbon and because of its originality and zest for life can be even more friendly.

A region to explore

Both in terms of scenery and culture the north has much to offer. Here you will find a colourful landscape of the most varied greens and browns, extensive areas of forest, and mountain ranges which, as in the Serra de Estrêla, can rise to a height of 1,993 m. There are the romantic river valleys of the Rio Douro and the Rio Cávado with their productive estates and tranquil beauty, while the coast has several pleasant seaside resorts. In addition there are the cultural strongholds such as Braga, the town of churches, which has earned the nickname of 'the Rome of Portugal'.

A holiday with a difference

The list of reasons why it should be worth while spending a holiday in the north is virtually endless, and this does not only apply to those who travel by car via Paris, San Sebastián and Vigo. However, if you are merely looking for a holiday by the sea or seeking the kind of activity which can be found in a modern holiday centre, you will probably not get your money's worth by coming here. On the other hand, if you have a car at your disposal and are anxious to discover something new, then you will have picked the right place, and this is particularly true if you are someone who derives enjoyment from the great variety of nature and culture. Moreover, the countryside is still relatively undisturbed by tourism and this is reflected in lower prices and, most of all, in the cordial welcome of the people.

Oporto Pop. 800,000 (including suburbs)

The British love Oporto (*Porto* in Portuguese), and not only because of its port wine. It has the kind of climate which the British are used to — a lot of mist and rain! But the metropolis of the north, and the second largest town in the country, has much more to offer. It has genuine Baroque architecture, churches of exceptional beauty and picturesque boats moored at the Douro quays. Like a huge natural amphitheatre the tightly packed houses in the old town, with their narrow little alleyways, cover the steep banks of the river. The towers of the cathedral and the *Torre dos Clérigos* look out over the red roofs of the houses with their gardens, terraces and flower-filled balconies, as far as *Vila Nova da Gaia*.

As a result of its position close to the mouth of the River Douro, Oporto remains today the most important trading centre in Portugal, next to Lisbon. Henry the Navigator's ships were built here in the dockyards and the residents of the time were forced to live on offal as all the available meat was salted down for the crews; even to this day the residents of Oporto are proud to be known as *Tripeiros* (offal eaters).

A town of contrasts

Industrial plants, oil refineries and the

busy harbour of Leixões, at the mouth of the Douro, make up the industrial centre of Oporto. It is a town of banks, of granite mansion houses built by rich merchants to last for ever, of jewellers and of goldsmiths. In contrast, however, this large town has many beggars, filthy children and pitifully dirty slums. Nevertheless, the churches, the university, and the proximity of the bathing beaches of *Foz de Douro* and *Leça de Palmeira* (though these tend to be crowded) all make Oporto into a town tourists should not miss. There is an international airport and also accommodation to suit every taste and pocket.

History

Oporto is among the oldest settlements in the country. As an inhabited town it can be traced back as far as the 5th c. and it became a cathedral city in the year A.D. 560. From A.D. 760 to 820 Oporto was occupied by the Moors, and then again from 825 to 868. It did not come under Christian rule until the year 1050. Oporto flourished during the Age of Discovery, was besieged by the French in 1808 during the Peninsular War and was relieved by Wellington in the following year.

New Town with port wine cellars

If you have time to spare and are not a teetotaller, a visit to *Vila Nova da Gaia*, the new quarter of Oporto, is recommended as a prelude to your sightseeing trip. Here are the many port wine cellars, in the vaults of which are stored the long rows of oak barrels, often hundreds of years old. Samples are readily offered!

It is not just the wine cellars which justify a visit to Vila Nova da Gaia, but also the view over the Douro of a large part of the old city. The most attractive square is the *Serra do Pilar* in front of the 16th c. convent *Mosteiro Nossa Senhora do Pilar*. Immediately next to it the bridge dedicated to *D. Luis I* (1881–1885) leads to the old quarter, the true heart of the city. The second bridge which spans the Douro is known as *Ponte Dona Maria Pia*, and was built in the year 1877 by Gustave Eiffel who also built the Eiffel Tower in Paris.

Old Town

First of all, stroll along the banks of the river through that part of the town called *Maragaia*, with its little 18th c. church *São Pedro*, its colourful streets and the old port wine boats on the river.

From Maragaia go by way of the *Cais de Ribeira*, where you can sit outside the numerous bars and cafés, to the busy fish market at *Praça da Ribeira*. Here you will find a small monument commemorating the worst accident in the history of Oporto. During the second invasion of Portugal by Napoleon's armies, 6,000 people lost their lives here in 1809 when the bridge collapsed.

A walk through the Old Town

It is best to begin a visit to the old *Cidade* at the *Praça do Município*, where the Tourist Information Office is situated in the Town Hall. Here you can obtain a very informative leaflet about the city. After strolling through a well tended park you will arrive at *Praça da Liberdade*, from where the *Rua dos Clérigos* winds steeply up to the church of the same name. The 75-m-high granite tower of this church is the tallest in the city and from the upper level there is a panoramic view. Passing on through the attractive gardens of *João Chagas* you come to the two Carmelite churches. The older one dates back to the early 17th c. and is embellished with beautiful tile work, while the other was built some 50 years later. A little beyond the *San António* Hospital is the *Museu Nacional de Soares dos Reis*, which is housed in the *Palácio dos Carrancas*, a royal palace dating back to the 18th c. Inside there is a large collection

Right: Oporto

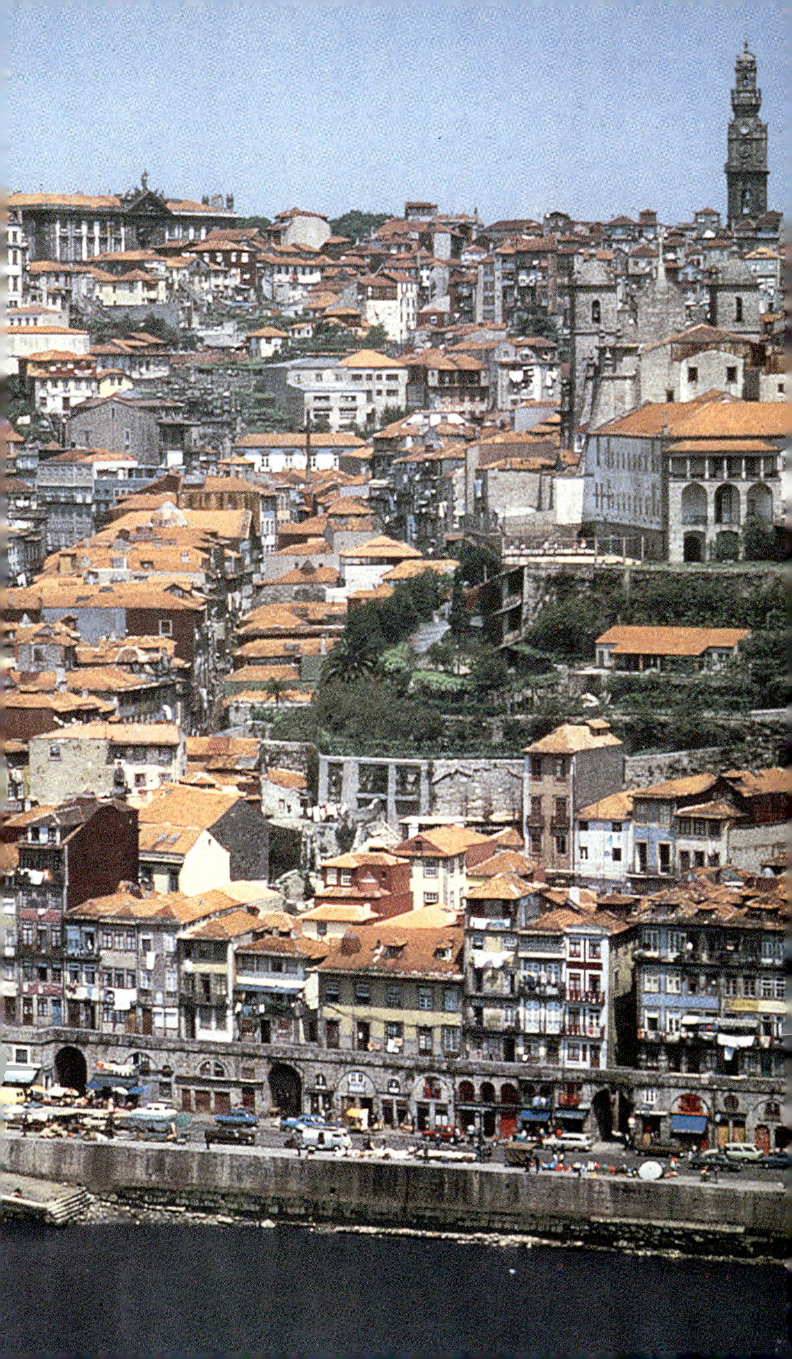

of prehistoric artefacts and an extensive series of paintings, sculptures, porcelain and goldsmiths' work from several centuries.

> **A special tip**
> A pleasant way of getting a general view of the city is to take a boat trip on the River Douro. These trips, which last for 40 minutes, take place between May and October. The point of departure is the Vila Nova da Gaia, the new town section of the city.

Now go down again to the real old part of the city as far as the 17th c. church of *São Bento da Vitória*, which has a very fine carved High Altar. From here you can either take a walk along the *Rua das Flores*, where you can buy lovely gold- or silverware and jewellery in the many little shops, or you can go further along towards the river until you reach the *Palácio da Bolsa*, the Stock Exchange. This 19th c. Classical style building was constructed on the site of a Franciscan monastery, which had been destroyed by fire. The pomp and ostentation of the rich Portuguese merchants is admirably expressed in the huge rooms heavily decorated with gold. Particularly delightful is the *Sala Arabe*, a banqueting hall which is still entirely in the Moorish style. Next to it stands the Baroque church of *São Francisco,* which was desecrated by Napoleon's soldiers and used as a stable. The interior of this church, which was built at the end of the 14th c., contains some exquisite wood carvings called *Talha Douradas*.

In the heart of the Old Town

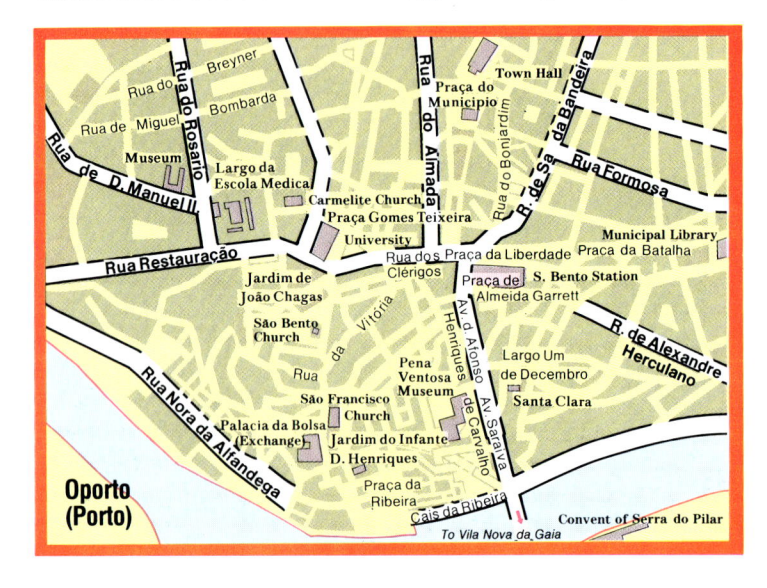

If you walk through the Ribeira part of the city, you will learn something of the other Oporto and get to know about the real Old Town. There are narrow alleys lined with crumbling façades, hosts of noisy children, shops of all kinds, some of which are most unusual, stores, cafés and bars, and everywhere the sounds of music, shouting children and yapping dogs. The Portuguese capital of Lisbon cannot offer anything to compare with this lively Old Town. On the edge of this maze of alleyways, narrow streets and steep flights of steps, at the point where a large market is held, rises *Penha Ventosa*, a hill on which stands the *Sé*, Oporto's cathedral. This Romanesque-Gothic fortress church was built in the 12th and 13th centuries and restored in the Baroque style in the 18thc. The Altar *do Sacramento* (17th c. with splendid silver work) in the side chapel *Capela-Mór,* and the 14th c. Gothic cloister, later decorated with 18thc. azulejos, are of particular interest.

The square on which the Sé stands is known as the *Terreiro da Sé* and from there you can get a good view over part of the Old Town and also of Vila Nova da Gaia on the other side of the Douro. Here also is the elaborate Pelourinho in Manueline style, as well as the 18thc. *Paço Episcopal*, the Episcopal Palace. A flea market is held every Saturday in the square. Just a little further on some steps lead to the *Os Grilos*, the first and, according to some connoisseurs, the best example in Portugal of a Baroque church. This Jesuit church dates from the beginning of the 17th c. A short distance further on you reach the former 15th c. convent chapel of *Santa Clara*. While the façade of this chapel is composed of a not too interesting mixture of Gothic and Renaissance features, the wonderful gilded-wood carvings in the interior contribute to the reputation of Santa Clara as one of the finest churches in Portugal. From here you can proceed to the *Praça da Batalha*, where stands a statue of King Pedro V and where the tile decorations in the Church of *Santo Ildefonso* are well worth seeing.

Abadia and *Montenegro*.

Fado bar *Mal Conzinhado* and *Cozinha Real do Fado*.

Interesting museums include the *Museu Guerra Junqueiro* with collections of furniture, tapestries, silver and porcelain from the 14th to the 18th centuries; and the *Museu Romantico e Solar do Vinho do Porto*, a museum devoted to the port wine trade; from here there is a fine view over the river and the New Town. Worth visiting is the *Palais Cristal*, a park with a good view over the town and with exhibitions, amusements and restaurants.

A folk-festival, celebrated mainly on the streets of the Old Town, takes place on June 23rd and 24th.

The Costa Verde and its Hinterland

Costa Verde, the 'Green Coast', is a very misleading term for the vast region in the extreme north of the country bordered by Oporto in the south, Vila Real in the east and Spain in the north. If you separate the two words, however, it does enable you to pin down the character of this region. On the one hand there is the coastal area, a vast, very fine stretch of sandy beach, with a large number of fishing villages and holiday resorts. On the other hand, the hinterland is one of the most interesting and varied regions in the whole of Portugal and it is, in fact, green.

Here it is the fruit orchards, the vineyards and the huge pine forests which determine the nature of the countryside. Along the Spanish border it is the fantastic but inhospitable rock formations of the Serra da Peneda and of the Serra do Gerês which are so impressive. Here variety is the operative word, even when it comes to the very good but almost unknown cuisine of this part of the country. Historical and artistic interests are also catered for on the Costa Verde. There are castles, fortresses, famous churches to which pilgrimages are made, and cathedrals.

In order really to get to know the Costa Verde it is a great advantage to have a car, especially if you choose as your base one of the old manorial country seats which take in guests and are known as *Casas Antigas*.

Vila do Conde Pop. 15,900

Situated on the mouth of the Rio Ave and overlooked by the Convent of *Santa Clara*, this tiny fishing village and seaside resort is only 4 km from Póvoa de Varzim. Still undiscovered by tourists, the town, in which a few spinning mills have become established, has a great deal to offer including wide stretches of sandy beach, broken up here and there by rocks. There is also the convent, founded in A.D. 1318, but which in its present form only goes back to the 18th c. It has an interesting church with a Manueline chapel and the tombs of its founders, Dom Afonso Sanches and his wife. The 15th c. parish church of São João was built by Basques from the Spanish side of the frontier.

Very peaceful with only one large hotel, *Estalagem do Brasão*.

Extensive beaches to the south of the town, in particular *Azurara* and *Arvore*.

To be built on the main beach, *Praia do Vila do Conde*.

A small town museum and the house of the poet José Régio who died in 1969. In the house there is a small collection of paintings.

Convent of Santa Clara, Vila do Conde

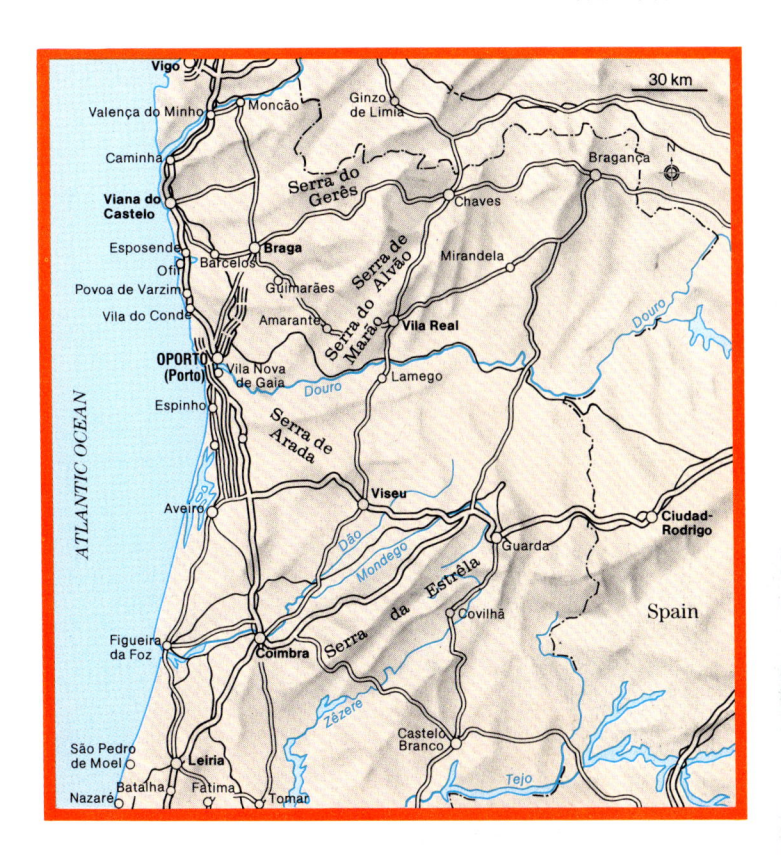

🍴 *Café Ao Bom Doce* with a great variety of regional cakes and pastries.

⛺ On the beach at Arvore.

🎉 *Feira do São João* from June 14th to 24th, a religious festival with processions and dancing, partly in national costume.

🚌 To the remains of a former aqueduct 7 km long, which was built in the 18th c.; to the hilltops of Santa Felix and *Monte de Santa Ana*, from which a good view of the countryside can be obtained, and to Póvoa de Varzim.

A special tip
In Rates, 15 km away, stands the Romanesque church of *São Pedro de Rates*, one of the oldest churches in Portugal. It was built at the beginning of the 12th c. by Count Dom Henrique. Of particular interest are the lovely main doorway and the south doorway.

Póvoa de Varzim Pop. 20,000
'.....and many people came to buy fish and to bathe in the sea'. These words are taken from the minutes of a Council Meeting held in 1776. The popularity of the town, situated 28 km north of

Oporto, on the Atlantic coast, still remains the same today. A great deal of building is taking place in the town itself, but this is most certainly compensated for by the picturesque fishing quarter and its fish market. There is an interesting hinterland which is worth a visit and there are plenty of places offering holiday accommodation.

A very long sandy beach, which is extremely clean.

On the beach and at the Hotel *Vermar Dom Pedro*.

Clube Navale Povoense.

Rifle range in the stadium.

Hotel Vermar Dom Pedro

In the majority of restaurants local specialities appear on the menu, for instance *Açorda de Mariscos*, a thick soup containing mussels.

Boite do Casino which has a nightclub and the Hotel Vermar Dom Pedro.

Casino (roulette) with music hall; from June to November, shows featuring international artistes.

Discothèque *Contempo*.

Embroidered knitwear, silver and filigree work (good value).

Two cinemas with international films in the original languages.

Regular football matches and, in August only, bullfights. The religious festival, *Feira do São Pedro*, takes place on June 28th to 29th.

The *Rancho Poveiro* folk troupe, organised by the Tourist Office.

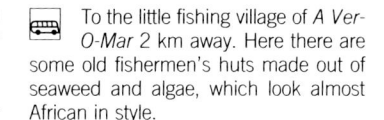

To the little fishing village of *A Ver-O-Mar* 2 km away. Here there are some old fishermen's huts made out of seaweed and algae, which look almost African in style.

Esposende-Ofir Pop. 24,350

The wide elongated mouth of the Rio Cávado divides Esposende from Fão-Ofir. The name of Ofir refers to the goldmines of King Solomon and it is this side of the town which will be of most interest to the tourist. Here you will find, situated among pinewoods by the sea and the estuary, a large choice of good hotels offering holiday accommodation. In Esposende the only historical sight worth visiting is the *Bonança* Chapel which is decorated with monograms and emblems of the fishermen.

For those who want to combine a relaxing holiday by the sea with exploring the northern area, Esposende-Ofir, because of its central position, is an ideal starting point.

The well spaced hotels and the peaceful atmosphere offer good opportunities for relaxation.

A kilometre away there are smooth sandy beaches on either side of the river mouth.

Hotels *de Ofir, do Pinhal, Estalagem Parque do Rio* in Ofir and *Suave-Mar* in Esposende.

Hotel de Ofir.

Children's swimming pool at the Hotel de Ofir.

Hotel de Ofir.

Hotels do Pinhal and de Ofir.

Hotel Suave-Mar.

Right: Lima River

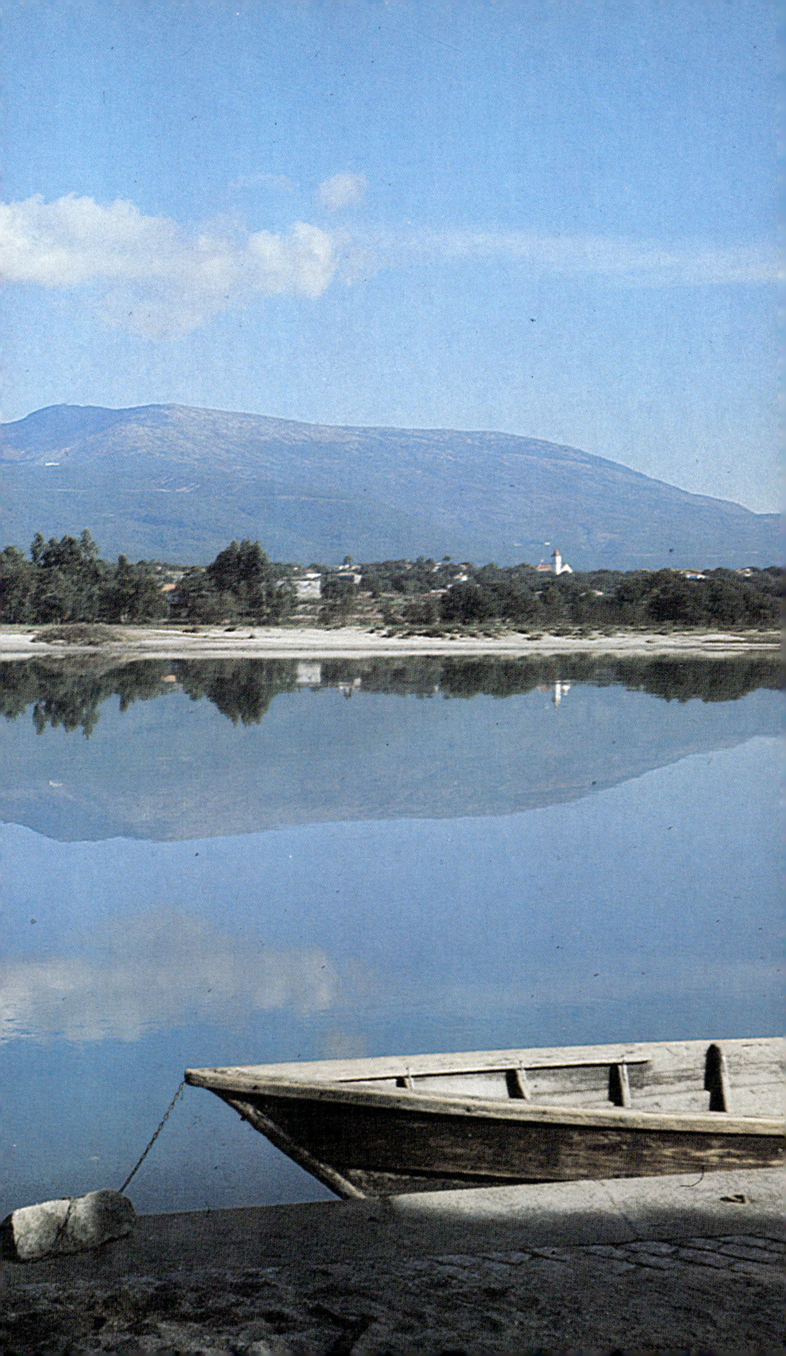

Costa Verde

> ✕ Hotels de Ofir and Suave-Mar.

> ♪ Hotel de Ofir and *Estalagem do Zende*.

> ▽ Hotel do Pinhal.

> 🚌 Along the beach to the little fishing village of *Apúlia*, 4 km away, where there are a few windmills and where you may be able to see some traditional kelp fishermen at work. In addition there are some small but quite good bars.

Into the interior, along the Rio Cávado through pine forests and vineyards, to the small but beautifully situated town of *São Bartolemeu do Mar,* a distance of about 6 km.

Viana do Castelo Pop. 18,000

It was the Romans who first described this town on the Atlantic Ocean at the mouth of the Rio Lima as *pulchra* (beautiful), and it remains so to this day. Across one of Gustave Eiffel's bridges is the really outstanding fishing harbour. The town's image is strongly influenced by its Renaissance and Baroque buildings. In the middle of the *Praça da República*, the centre of the town, stands a 16th c. fountain created by João Lopes. This square is regarded as one of the finest in the whole of the north. On it stands the former Town Hall and the 16th c. *Casa da Câmara*, a building with covered arcades. Here also can be found the *Misericórdia*, a 16th c. Renaissance building, and the *Misericórdia Church*, which is decorated with beautiful 18th c. tiles. Further places of interest are the former cloistered convent of *Santa Ana* dating from the 16th c., with a Moorish tower, and the late 16th c. Renaissance church *São Domingos*. 5 km outside the town you can get a wonderful view of the coast and of the town itself from the *Monte de Santa Luzia*, which has a church of the same name and also a hotel.

Viana do Castelo

A special tip
Unusual meals can be obtained at the *Santonhio Farm*, on the outskirts of the town. Every Saturday evening a typical Portuguese dish is served in traditional style at this old country house. It is advisable to book early.

> 🅁 The peaceful, pleasant atmosphere in the town guarantees a really relaxing holiday.

> ⛱ The *Cabedelo*, an extensive sandy beach with gentle dunes, is about 2 km from the centre of the town.

> 🎣 ♪ S 🛩
> 🤸 🏊 🔍
> ● ⛎

> ◨ Three times a week in Viana there is a film at the cinema or a performance at the theatre.

> ☂ The town museum is housed in an 18th c. mansion where, in particular, you can see some remarkable azulejos.

> ♪ Several discothèques.

> 🎸 There are folk music performances every Saturday.

> 🐂 Bullfights take place in August.

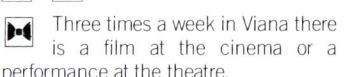

Caminha Pop. 2,000

This small village lies on the Rio Minho which separates Portugal from Spain, and consequently occupied a position of great strategic importance in earlier times. A fort remains today, situated on an island opposite the village of Caminha. The ruins of a 14th c. castle and of the 15th c. Gothic *Pilas Palace* testify to the long history of the town.

Also of interest is the late 15th c. parish church *Igreja Matriz*, with its Moorish wooden ceiling. The countryside is unspoilt and, because it has not been opened up by tourism, there are only a few pensions.

- Perfect for those looking for peace and solitude.
- Sandy beach and sand dunes stretching for over a kilometre.
- In a pine-wood just outside the town.
- Through the vast pine forests and along the beach.

Igreja Matriz, Caminha

Valença do Minho Pop. 3,000

This old frontier town on the river Minho does not possess any major treasures of art history. Nevertheless visitors to Portugal, especially those coming from northern Spain, should try to travel via Valença. It has a perfectly preserved fortress occupying a position overlooking the river, and among the sleepy alleyways of the town there are several secluded wine bars where a choice Vinho Verde may be sampled.

Espigueiros (grain stores), Minho

Monção Pop. 2,000

In the 17th c. Monção was an important stronghold but today hardly a vestige of the old splendour remains, although a stroll through its attractive little streets would be rewarding. There are two particular pleasures which no visitor should miss: this region is one of the most important wine-producing areas in Portugal and the best Vinho Verde in the

Monção

country comes from Monção; and some of the finest freshwater fish can be found here.

▲ On the banks of the Minho.

H Thermal springs in the *António Pinho* park.

🚌 To the *Palácio de Brejoeira*, a castle built in the 19th c., 7 km away.

Caldas do Gerês Alt. 400 m; Pop. 500

This village nestles in the deep valley of the Rio Gerês and was well known as far back as ancient Roman times for its thermal springs. Nowadays the peaceful little village is still visited by those wishing to benefit from the healing powers of the spa waters, and also by nature-lovers, on account of the magnificent landscape in which it is situated. In the village itself there are a few old-English style hotels.

⇌ Public swimming pool and at the Hotel *Parque*.

⌕ In the grounds of the Spa.

U At the riding stables in the National Park, 2 km away.

H Medicinal thermal springs and solarium.

🚌 Gerês lies on the edge of the *Parque Nacional da Peneda-Gerês*, which is a nature reserve covering an area of 70,000 hectares. This national park with its deep valleys, fast-running rivers, waterfalls, lakes, undisturbed villages and fantastic, almost unreal, rocky scenery, must assuredly be one of the most beautiful regions in the whole of Europe.

The park itself is divided into three zones. The outer zone in which Gerês is situated is quite accessible and may be visited by car. The intermediate zone of the park, where the excavations of an old Roman road can be seen, can only be explored on foot or by taking part in an organised tour. Camping in this zone is not allowed but a few years ago work began on the improvement of facilities for hikers and bird-watchers. There are over 50 hides available for bird-watchers, and hikers may spend the night in one of the several huts which have been completed. The inner zone is not open to the public. Information may be obtained from the Parque Nacional da Peneda-Gerês office in Gerês.

Braga Pop. 50,000 approx.

In the 5th century A.D. Braga became the first seat of government of the Suevian Empire. Next to Lisbon, Oporto and Coimbra this city on the Rio Minho is still considered to be one of the most important in the country. The Archbishop Primate of Portugal has his seat in Braga. In the same way that the business magnates of Oporto moulded the character of that city, so it was the high dignitaries of the church who made Braga into what it is today. Known as the 'town of churches', it is without doubt dominated by the *Sé*, the great cathedral which dates back to the 12th c. The south doorway and parts of the main doorway are the only remaining evidence of its Romanesque origins. Numerous extensions and renovations carried out at later dates have produced a mixture of Gothic, Manueline and Baroque styles. This is why the cathedral should be looked at in fine detail rather than as a complete whole. The tombs of Henry of Burgundy and his wife, Tareja, the parents of the first king of Portugal, can be seen in the cathedral. Both the 16th c. octagonal baptismal font and the side chapel of *São Pedro de Rates*, with some very fine 17th c. azulejos, are worth seeing, and you should also try to visit the Treasury Vault and the Museum of Religious Art.

Among the city's other places of interest are the former Bishop's Palace and the very attractive garden which adjoins it, the *Jardim Santa Bárbara*. In

Braga itself there is just one international hotel, the *Turismo*, which has a swimming pool and a discothèque.

🚌 *Bom Jesus do Monte*, a famous place of pilgrimage, lies 6 km to the west of Braga. Its late Baroque church was erected at the end of the 18th c. on the site of a former pilgrim church, and is one of the best-known places of pilgrimage in the country. An extensive flight of steps leads up to the Church of Bom Jesus, which stands at the end of a semicircular site on which are eight statues of biblical characters set on massive pedestals. On the way up the steps you pass twelve chapels, each depicting a Station of the Cross. The best view is to be had from the middle terrace. If you do not fancy walking up there is a lift which is still operated by water-power, or you can drive up the hill which is over 300 m in height. In the village near the church there are three hotels (one of four-star standard), and tennis courts. Long walks may be taken through the beautiful wooded countryside along well tended paths.

Barcelos Pop. 5,000.

Situated almost exactly half-way between Viana do Castelo and Guimarães, Barcelos is best known for its pottery, particularly the brightly painted cockerel which has become a tourist symbol for Portugal.

As a town which was at the height of its influence during the 14th and 15th centuries, Barcelos has a number of interesting historic buildings. The ruins of the palace of the dukes of Bragança have been converted into an open-air archaeological museum; here you can see a stone cross which is over 400 years old and on which the legend of the cockerel has been inscribed. The same building houses the second museum of this little town, the Museum of Ceramics, and next to it stands the Romanesque parish church, the oldest church in Barcelos, which dates from the 12th c.

Barcelos cockerels

Around the large Square of the Republic are three other churches, all of which repay a visit. These are the 17th c. Baroque church of *Bom Jesus da Cruz*, the 18th c. former monastery chapel of *Nossa Senhora do Terço*, which is decorated with large azulejo mosaics and has several ceiling paintings, and the *Misericórdia* Church which is also of 18th c. date.

Barcelos is reputed to be the skilled craft centre of northern Portugal. This is confirmed by the market, the largest in the north, which is held every Thursday, when pottery, embroidery, ceramics, objets d'art and household goods are offered for sale. Mention should also be made of the folk festival, *Romaria das Cruzes*, which takes place on May 3rd each year and features beautiful floral displays.

Chaves Pop. 15,000

The ancient Romans came to Chaves, on the Rio Tâmega, in order to take advantage of the thermal springs. They constructed the earliest fortifications in the town as well as a bridge with twelve arches, which was part of a road from

Typical verandahs — Chaves

Braga to Asturias, and which has now been completely restored. In the course of time Chaves developed into a stronghold of the dukes of Bragança and in the 15th c. it served as their main seat of residence. Most things of interest to be seen here today go back largely to the 17th c. The Baroque *Misericórdia* Church, the interior of which is panelled with azulejos, and the Romanesque former parish church are both situated in the attractive old town. However, if you come here for thermal treatment you could well be disappointed; a much more satisfactory place would be, the little town of Vidago which is only 17 km away.

Bragança Alt. 684 m; Pop. 9,000

This town on the northern edge of the *Serra de Nogueira* is the home of the last Portuguese royal palace. As a sturdy frontier fortress town, Bragança played a crucial role in the Middle Ages. Towering above the old houses in this picturesque little town is a large citadel. You will find almost all Bragança's more important buildings in the upper part of the town.

The most historical is the former Town Hall, the *Domus Municipalis*. This five-sided 13th c. Romanesque building is the only secular building of this period in Portugal and is considered to be one of the finest in the whole of the Iberian peninsula.

In addition there is the 16th c. Renaissance Church of *Santa Maria*, the 15th c. military tower of *Torre de Menagem* and the Gothic pillory (pelourinho). The *Citadel*, which was constructed at the beginning of the 13th c. with double walls and 18 massive towers, was always thought to be impregnable. In 1808 during the Peninsular War the first revolt broke out here against the army of Junot, the Napoleonic general.

In the town itself there are only a few historic buildings of any significance, the most interesting being, without doubt, the Renaissance cathedral with its magnificent doorway.

Guimarães Pop. 20,000

In A.D. 1140, the first king of Portugal,

Cathedral, Bragança

Bragança

Afonso Henriques, chose as his capital city Guimarães, the place of his birth. The huge castle in which he is said to have been born is the town's landmark. Just as interesting as the castle, however, is the Church of *Nossa Senhora da Oliveira*, a former monastery chapel, dating back to the 10th c. Other places of interest include the palace of the dukes of Bragança, which was built in Gothic style at the beginning of the 15th c., the 16th c. Town Hall on the *Largo I Maio*, and the *Rua de Santa Maria*, a lovely old street.

The town has two notable museums, one of which, the *Museu Alberto de Sampaio*, is well known for its paintings, wood carvings, altar vestments and sacred works of art in gold. This museum is housed in the former monastery building *da Oliveira* with its Romanesque cloisters which are worth seeing. The other museum, *Museu Martins Sarmento*, is an archaeological museum containing predominantly Celtic artefacts.

To *Citânia Briteiros*, 10 km away, where there are ruins of a Celtic village dating from the 5th c. B.C. They are situated on a hilltop from which there is a superb view over the surrounding country. Into the *Serra de Santa Caterina*, a mountain chain which rises to 580 m, 17 km from Guimarães, in the mountains, stands the pilgrim church of *Nossa Senhora da Penha*, from where there are also some wonderful views.

Amarante Pop. 5,000

The little town of Amarante lies at the foot of the Serra do Marão amidst very rugged scenery, on the banks of the Rio Tâmega. There is a small swimming pool and a camping site quite near the river. Apart from the *São Gonçalo Monastery*, which was built at the beginning of the 16th c., and its church with the so-called 'King's Lodge', there is very little else of any significance.

27 km from the town of Amarante at a height of 900 m is the *Pousada de São Gonçalo*, where guests are offered first-class Portuguese specialist dishes. In 1986 the surrounding forest was unfortunately almost completely destroyed by fire. The re-afforestation of the area is going ahead, but slowly, and consequently opportunities for walking have been severely limited. Excursions to both the *Alto do Espinho*, which at 1,020 m is the highest point in the mountain range, and to the Rio Corgo Valley are worth while.

Home of the Mateus family

From the Douro to the Tagus

That region of Portugal which lies between the River Douro in the north and the Mondego in the south is known mainly to wine connoisseurs. The little Rio Dão flows almost exactly through the middle of the region which produces the most celebrated of the Portuguese wines. Many tourists, whether travelling from Spain or heading north from Lisbon, tend to visit Oporto and to ignore this part of the country. By doing so they miss the gentle slopes and the more rugged beauty of ever-changing mountain scenery. In this region there are vast forests, fertile valleys and a very interesting part of the coast, the Costa de Prata. By comparison with the coast north of Oporto water temperatures in this area are more favourable and the sea more inviting for bathers.

With Lisbon and Oporto, Coimbra completes the triumvirate of fine cities in Portugal. It is a lovely old city which, because of its art and its history, has played an important role in the life of Portugal. As well as Coimbra, Viseu, Aveiro, Óbidos, Batalha and Tomar are all worth visiting.

Seaside Resorts

Espinho Pop. 12,000

The industrial town and seaside resort of Espinho lies 20 km south of Oporto at the mouth of the Rio Largo. It boasts nothing of historical importance other than the fact that it is laid out in chequered fashion, after the manner of the old colonial towns. Its popularity as a resort and a tourist town is now increasing as a result of an extensive building programme and its large-scale sporting and entertainment facilities.

Extensive beach to the north and to the south of the town.

Right: The beach at Nazaré

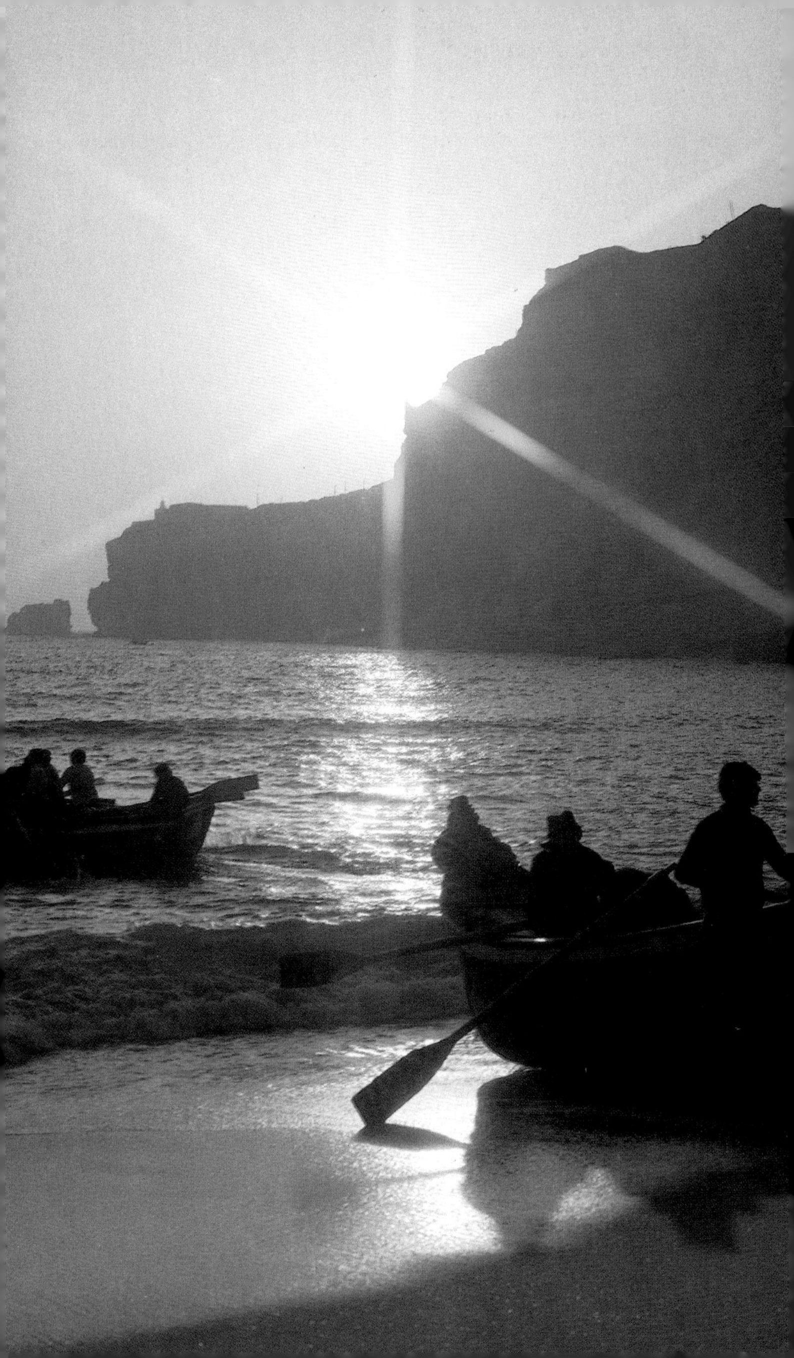

Youth hostel, Aveiro

Between Douro and Minho, home of Vinho Verde.

- ⛱ Large swimming pool right on the beach.
- 🏌 *Oporto Golf Club*, 2 km outside the town, has an 18-hole course.
- 🔍 *Parque João de Deus*.
- ✒ Oporto Golf Club.
- 🅰 🛼 🎿 🎵
- ⊗ Hotel *Praia Golfe*
- 🍴 Casa Zagabo
- 🎪 Numerous events, gymkhanas, air shows, traditional processions and musical festivals are held at varying times during the year.

Aveiro Pop. 25,000

The Portuguese compare Aveiro, an old fishing and seaport town situated on the estuary of the Rio Vouga, with Venice. The town, lying on the eastern edge of a long stretch of lagoons and intersected by canals, really does have a southern flavour about it. In fact, the countryside also reminds you of the former Zuiderzee in Holland. Colourful fishing craft and sailing boats, and ox carts waiting in front of the dazzlingly white salt works, all make for a perfect scene. Aveiro has a large number of historically interesting buildings. The most important ones are the *Convento de Jesus* where the Regional Museum is situated, and where some magnificent gilded wood-panelling and carvings can be seen in the chapel, and the cathedral with its Gothic cloisters. The *Misericórdia* Church, probably designed

Grape-harvesting ox carts

Windmills of Estremadura

by Filippe Terzi, has a richly decorated main doorway and is also of considerable interest.

A special tip

Of unequalled beauty is the huge lagoon known as *Ria* comprising creeks, canals and small lakes. The salt workings, the cod fishing fleet in the harbour at *Gafanha* and the region of the *Moliceiros*, where seaweed gathering is still carried on, may be visited by boat.

Aveiro is a real holiday town and is ideal as a starting point for trips on the lakes.

The sandy beaches of *Barra, Costa Nova* and *S. Jacinto* are bounded by sand dunes and are quite easy to reach by bus or by boat. The gently sloping beaches on the lagoon are ideal for children.

The Rio Vouga, the lagoon and the Atlantic ocean offer good opportunities for fishing enthusiasts.

The shooting of waterfowl on the lagoon is allowed between August 15th and March 15th.

Ceramics, model boats and confectionery, especially *Ovos Moles*, egg sweets in little wooden barrels.

Figueira da Foz Pop. 12,000

Cod fishing has made Figueira da Foz, with its picturesque harbour, into a wealthy little town. It lies at the mouth of the Rio Mondego and is the most popular seaside resort on the west coast of Portugal but, in spite of that, it has not become overcrowded. The sleepy, narrow alleys in the old town blend well with the wide roads and modern hotels to be found on the coast and around the harbour. Well worth seeing is the *Paço da Figueira*, originally a seat of the nobility, which is decorated with exactly 6,888 Delft tiles.

A 3-km-long sandy beach, *Praia da Claridade*.

At the Figueira Tennis Club.

There are several homely restaurants in the old town offering favourably priced fish dishes.

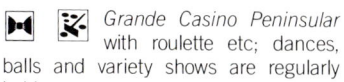

Grande Hotel and *Estalagem da Piscina*.

Grande Casino Peninsular with roulette etc; dances, balls and variety shows are regularly held.

Two cinemas and a large pleasure park.

Bullfights, sporting events and folk music concerts often take place.

Walks in the *Serra da Boa Viagem* and on the *Mondego Headland*.

Trips to Coimbra (44 km) and Conimbriga (40 km).

São Pedro de Moel Alt. 0–50 m; Pop. 1,000

The margraves of Vila Real and the dukes of Caminha all enjoyed staying in this seaside town which is situated 30 km north of Nazaré. It is a holiday resort with aristocratic traditions and is neither overrun by tourists nor over-expensive. The town lies in the centre of the famous pine forests of Leiria which were established in the 13th and 14th centuries. Apart from two large hotels, *Mar e Sol* and *São Pedro de Moel*, there are a number of guest houses as well as a government-sponsored pousada.

Because of its peaceful, remote position, São Pedro is able to offer restful holidays for those seeking relaxation. Entertainment facilities are negligible.

A large, clean sandy beach behind which is an extensive pine forest.

A large, modern swimming pool complex right on the beach with a good restaurant, bar etc.

In the town, the *Bambi*; just outside the town, the *Mina*.

In the Hotel *Mar e Sol*.

During the season films are shown at the swimming complex.

Portuguese cuisine is available at the *Pai dos Frangos*.

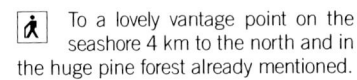

To a lovely vantage point on the seashore 4 km to the north and in the huge pine forest already mentioned.

To Batalha (30 km), Nazaré (30 km) and Fátima (50 km).

Nazaré Alt. 5–110 m; Pop. 10,000

This picturesque fishing village, shielded against the north wind by the foothills of the *Sítio* promontory, has for a long time been a favourite holiday spot for French tourists visiting Portugal. For those who know just how much the French treasure good food and an exhilarating holiday atmosphere, this is recommendation enough, and here you will find hotels and guest houses to suit every pocket. In addition Nazaré is a typical example of an old Portuguese town with traditional fishing methods and other genuine old customs (traditional costume is worn every day), and, not surprisingly, the town is very popular as a centre for day trips.

The shape of the fishing boats, with their high prows and the 'eye of God which helps in the search for fish' painted on each side, is said to be of Phoenician origin. The fishermen of Nazaré, where there is neither harbour nor jetty, push their boats into the sea, often through heavy breakers, to do their fishing, and, when they are fully laden, pull them back again on to the sandy beach using ox carts or tractors, or sometimes by hand, with a ritualistic rhythm known as *arte xavega*. Here the sorting and packing of the catch, which usually includes a lot of swordfish, takes place as it is prepared for its journey to the market.

From the beach at the lower part of the town, a cable car and a steep flight of steps between the rocks and agaves lead to that part of the town known as Sítio, situated on a very high steep cliff. Following his voyage to India, Vasco da Gama made a pilgrimage to the Memorial Chapel at the top of this cliff. A more recently built pilgrim church here contains a shrine to Nossa Senhora da Nazaré.

Extensive beaches of fine golden-yellow sand, bordered in the north by steep cliffs. In the high season the

Between Douro and Tagus 81

beaches become very crowded.

🍴 Several fish restaurants where you can get good value for money; bars and street cafés.

♪ *Virgula* and *Scotch*.

🍷 Several bars where you can have a lively time.

🎸 Frequent performances of folk music with dancing; fishermen's songs presented in a traditional manner.

🎪 During the second week in September there is a church festival in honour of Our Lady of Nazaré, with a procession and a fair.

🧺 Woollen knitwear.

🚶 To the lighthouse at *Sítio* and to the *São Bras* hill from both of which there are panoramic views. To the caves and rocks of *Forna da Orça*.

🚌 To Alcobaça (14 km); Batalha (35 km); Óbidos (37 km); Fátima (55 km), and Peniche (60 km) (see under São Martinho).

São Martinho do Porto Alt. 0–80 m; Pop. 1,600.

This town, situated approximately 100 km north of Lisbon, is developing into a thriving holiday resort. Its peace, however, can be broken by the extensive building programme being carried on.

🏖 Clean, very smooth, sandy beach with cliffs on either side of the wide bay. Good facilities for water-sports.

🔍 At the Hotel *do Parque*.

S 🏄 🏊 🚣

👶 Beach is safe for children.

♪ 🍷 Discothèque and bar in the Hotel do Parque. Nightclubs *Feeling* and *Bonny e Clyde*.

⛺ On the beach.

🚌 To Nazaré (12 km); Alcobaça (20 km); Óbidos (24 km); Peniche (approx. 50 km). Peniche is situated on a peninsula and has a large castle. 3 km away is the *Cabo Carvoeiro*, with needles of rock rising out of the sea and a magnificent view from the top of the

Drying sardines in the sun at Nazaré

cliffs. The luxurious *Casa Abaiga*, for which advance booking is advisable, occupies the casemates of the old fort on the main island of the *Berlanga* group. It is about an hour's journey by boat from Peniche and the return fare is 250 Esc. There is a camping site, the ruins of a monastery, footpaths to caves, grottoes and cliffs, and excellent facilities for anglers, deep-sea fishermen and divers.

The Hinterland

Santarém Pop. 25,000.

The capital of the lower Tagus region, 50 km south-east of Leiria and 80 km north-east of Lisbon, Santarém is today a modern industrial and commercial city. In the old town centre, however, there are several places of interest.

The vantage point of *Portas do Sol*, situated on the steep bank of the Tagus, affords a magnificent view over Santarém and the surrounding area. The Archaeological Museum, which contains a wealth of exhibits, has under its roof the highly ornate tomb of Dom Duarte de Menezes as well as an elegant choir ambulatory from the Domingo Monastery. The *Graça* Church is a Gothic masterpiece and the *De Marvila* Church is distinguished by a particularly fine Manueline doorway. The Jesuit college on Bandeira Square has an impressive façade and interesting tile mosaics in the corridors.

Óbidos Alt. 70–150 m; Pop. 6,000.

Visitors are immediately impressed by this picturesque little town, dating back to the Middle Ages, which is set above the Rio Vargem in the region of Leiria. If you go through the *Porta da Vila*, the town gate, where a market is held every morning, you come to the heart of Óbidos which is surrounded by 13-m-high walls which go back to Moorish times.

Numerous towers complete with battlements break the severity of the walls. The well restored castle, which is worth visiting, is a splendid example of medieval architecture. Where in earlier times the noblemen of Portugal sat at table, tourists can today enjoy first-class food, choice wines and Portuguese hospitality, as the castle has been turned into a pousada. It is not just keen photographers who will enjoy a walk through Óbidos. In picturesque flower-filled streets, lanes and alleyways there are large numbers of fine mansions with beautiful Renaissance and Baroque façades. You should visit the Church of *Santa Maria* on the main square of the town, as the entire building is adorned with azulejos. There is also a beautifully decorated pelourinho. Inside the church can be seen a monument to the Governor of Óbidos which was made by Jean de Rouen. Diagonally across the square from the church stands the small town museum.

It is very rare to find a genuine article in any of the antique shops here. Not much time is required to visit Óbidos but the town is nevertheless worth seeing. If you want to spend more than one day here there is a four-star hotel, the *Estalagem do Convento*, and also a pension, the *Mansão da Torre,* which lies just outside the town.

Alcobaça Pop. 5,000.

Overlooked by the ruins of a Moorish castle, the town of Alcobaça lies 41 km south-east of Nazaré and 21 km south-west of Batalha. The central point of an extensive region, it would be of little significance at all for tourists were it not for the large Monastery of *Santa Maria*. This is one of the most important buildings of the early Gothic period. It is true that it contains later additions in the Manueline, Renaissance and Baroque styles, and that much was destroyed by both earthquake and the Peninsular War, but a splendid overall impression still remains. In addition to the dignified, plain, almost pure Gothic church interior (note the tombs of Pedro I and Ines de Castro) there are also the Gothic-Manueline cloisters and the library. Nowadays this is empty but its proportions are admirable. The Royal Hall, with its azulejos representing scenes from the history of the monastery, is also worthy of mention.

Good-class antiques, fine pillow-lace, beautiful white and blue pottery and other craftwork can be found in a number of shops on the Church Square and in the adjacent side streets. Friday is market day.

Fátima Pop. 6,450.

On October 13th 1917 70,000 almost hysterical people witnessed the 'Dance of the Sun'. A miracle had happened and the Virgin Mary had appeared with her call for peace. Even if peace had not come to the world, this small village was given an immense boost. Prior to 1917 Fátima could not be found on any map but, apart from Lourdes, it has become the best-known place of pilgrimage in Europe. Pilgrims come from all over the world into this once quiet little place and provide local tradesmen with a good income from their sales of religious material.

It all began with a vision witnessed by three children who, on May 13th 1917, were tending sheep on the hillside of *Cova da Iria*. The Virgin Mary appeared to them on five occasions. The Pope acknowledged the miracle, a shrine was erected and the pilgrims came in their hundreds of thousands. Pilgrimages on a large scale take place on the 13th of each month, especially in May and October. The shrine itself with its neo-Classical portico is, however, an ostentatious building completely lacking in style.

Leiria Pop. 29,000

This town where two important roads cross, south of Coimbra, is overlooked by the 12th–14th c. Royal Palace which is situated on a hilltop. Also worth seeing are the 17th c. cathedral, the 12th c. Church of *São Pedro*, the 16th c. pilgrimage church and the museum.

Batalha Pop. 7,000

Forget about the town of Batalha. Just concentrate on the Monastery of *Santa Maria de Vitória*, which was founded by King João I on the strength of a vow made after the victorious Battle of Aljubarrota against the Spaniards. From 1388 to 1533 work was carried out on the construction of this monastery, the most important in Portugal. Following extensive damage caused by the earthquake of 1755 and later by French troops, the monastery was carefully restored between 1840 and 1965.

The monastery church, with its imposing west front and its main entrance with sixfold articulation, is one of the most magnificent late Gothic masterpieces in Europe. In the interior of the church, notice the chancel window, which dates back to the 16th c., the star-shaped cupola and the filigree rosette in the founder's chapel. In addition there are the graves of Henry the Navigator and of several kings. The chapter house is impressive for its vaulted roof which has no intermediary supports and for its stained glass windows. The transition from the Gothic to the Manueline styles of architecture is reflected in the ornamentation of the 'Royal Cloister' and of the 'Unfinished Chapels'.

Tomar Pop. 16,000

The cross and the sword have shaped the history of this charming town which lies on the banks of the Rio Nabão, 30 km to the east of Fátima. It was the Knights Templar and then the Knights of Christ who first made their mark on Tomar, but that was not enough, and these valiant servants of God proceeded to make world history. Their emblem, the red Maltese cross, was depicted on

Tomar Rotunda — a unique example

the sails of every caravel which sailed to bring world power to Portugal. The character of the town is reflected in the narrow winding alleyways, the large squares and the splendid, well maintained façades. Of the town's churches, emphasis must be placed on the *São João Baptista*, with its fine Manueline doorway and an interior which is well worth seeing, and the Gothic *Santa Maria do Olival*, the burial place of many distinguished members of the Order of the Knights of Christ.

Tomar, however, is dominated by the *Convento de Cristo*, a Crusaders' castle and a convent all in one, which rises majestically over the town. This building, constructed by the Knights of Christ, is the largest combined castle and convent in Portugal. Work which was begun on the building in the 12th c. was not completed until the 17th. Dating back to the 12th c. and of particular note are the famous Rotunda, Henry the Navigator's palace with a two-storeyed arcaded courtyard, King Manuel's *Santa Barbara* cloister and the more recent chapter house. The convent itself, with its Cloister *dos Filippos*, was constructed at the behest of King João III and is the largest Renaissance building in Portugal. Fine examples of Manueline architecture and sculpture can be found in the reconstructed entrance of the Templars' Rotunda (architect João de Castilho) and in the famous window of the Santa Barbara Cloister which is the work of Diego de Arruda.

Every two years (1988, 1990 etc.) in July the *Tabuleiros* Festival is celebrated. It lasts for four days and there is a procession followed by folk-dancing and fireworks.

Almorol

This island in the middle of the River Tagus, 25 km south of Tomar, with a 12th c. Templars' castle, must surely be one of the most romantic places in Portugal. A well maintained perimeter wall, flanked by ten round towers, surrounds a high keep from where there is a very good view. If you take a boat trip it is possible to get a splendid photograph of the castle from the river. (Boats go from the north bank of the Tagus.)

Castelo Branco Alt. 470 m; Pop. 25,000

This regional capital on the edge of the Tagus plain lies close to the Spanish border. Sightseeing in the town, which is surrounded by olive groves, is worth while, as is a visit to the Baroque Episcopal Garden *(Jardim Episcopal)* with its many statues.

Coimbra Pop. 56,000

Coimbra is reputed to be one of the finest cities in the country. Positioned in a natural amphitheatre on the right bank of the Rio Mondego, it is closely linked with the growth and development of Portugal. Not only is it a city with tradition, but it is also a modern and industrial one which has come to terms with progress without losing any of its charm. As the seat of the first and for centuries the only university in Portugal, Coimbra has considerably influenced

University of Coimbra

the art and culture of the country. For a long time the image of students sombrely dressed in black was imprinted on the character of the city and Coimbra earned the reputation of being the only place in Portugal where any serious learning went on. But all that seems to be in the past now for, as in almost every university town, there are occasional student demonstrations in Coimbra and the sombre clothes have disappeared.

Coimbra was an important town even in the days of Imperial Rome, when it was known as Aeminium. In the year A.D. 716 the Moors seized this military base, but lost it again to the Portuguese in 1064. After Guimarães, Coimbra became the capital of the new kingdom, until King Afonso III moved the seat of government to Lisbon in the year 1260.

Coimbra consists of two parts, the upper and lower towns. There are a number of churches of significance in the 'Baixa', the lower part of Coimbra, but of particular interest is the *Mosteiro Santa Cruz*.

In the 12th and 13th centuries this once huge monastery was the cultural centre of Coimbra, and it was rebuilt by King Manuel in the style named after him. Most noteworthy are the choir stalls, carved in 1505, which illustrate the voyages of discovery made by Vasco da Gama, the graceful pulpit and the magnificent royal tombs in the chancel. Do have a look at the two-storeyed cloister, in the middle of which stands a perfectly shaped Renaissance fountain.

Also in the lower town you will find the elegant 16th c. palace of *Sobre Ripas* and the old cathedral. This is a Romanesque fortress church, the focal point of which must undoubtedly be the High Altar, made in 1508 by the Flemish master Oliver of Ghent.

For those interested in art history Santa Cruz Monastery may be the most important place, but the real Coimbra has yet to be seen. The atmosphere of the student town can only be felt in the upper part of Coimbra. Narrow, steep, picturesque little alleyways, cosy cafés and restaurants and small cheap wine taverns all contribute to a feeling of exuberance. This part of the town, indeed the whole of Coimbra, is dominated by the *Cidade Universitaria*. The size and architectural harmony of the old university complex are impressive in themselves, but there are also two particular buildings within it which are worthy of note. The first is the historic Library, consisting of three rooms, which is Baroque in its highest form and very like the court library by Fischer von Erlach in Vienna. (There is a good view of the city and the Mondego Valley from the balcony next to the library.) The other is the magnificent 16th c. Manueline university chapel.

Close to the university stands the late Baroque New Cathedral and the *Museu Machado de Castro*. This museum is in the former episcopal palace and has a Renaissance balcony from which there is a wonderful view over the roofs of Coimbra's old town. Displayed in the museum are some important antiquities, gold- and silverware and valuable paintings. On the other side of the Mondego you can see a modern-day spectacle — *Portugal dos Pequeninos* — a Portugal in miniature for children and grown-ups alike. Here there are plastic models of the principal buildings and representations of traditional scenes. Close to the miniature Portugal and at the top of the *Monte do Esperança* stands the Convent of *Santa Clara-a-Nova* where you can see the tomb of Saint Isobel, Queen of Portugal, who is the patron saint of Coimbra and is known as the *Rainha Santa*. The convent balcony commands the best panorama of Coimbra.

15 km south of Coimbra are the remains of the Roman settlement of *Conimbriga*. The whole area, which is very large and quite impressive, has well preserved thermal baths, the ruins of some fine Roman houses and the most splendid display of mosaics in the whole of the Iberian peninsula.

Viseu Alt. 483 m; Pop. 26,000

This town which was once a Roman fort has a vivid history. Since the year A.D. 569 it has been a cathedral town. In 1123 Dom Henriques took up residence and it was from here that he delivered his Constitutional Charter to the people. The town was also the birthplace of King Duarte.

All the historically important buildings are concentrated in the old town which is very picturesque and well preserved, having numerous splendid mansions, winding alleys and little squares. The visitor may see the remains of the 15th c. fortifications and the two surviving gates, *Porta do Cavaleiros* and *Porta do Soar*. There is also the *Misericórdia* Church, a Baroque building with an attractive façade, the cathedral, and the *Grão Vasco* Museum in a 16th c. palace which, together with examples of the goldsmith's art, contains a collection of paintings by Grão Vasco.

Right: Serra da Estrela

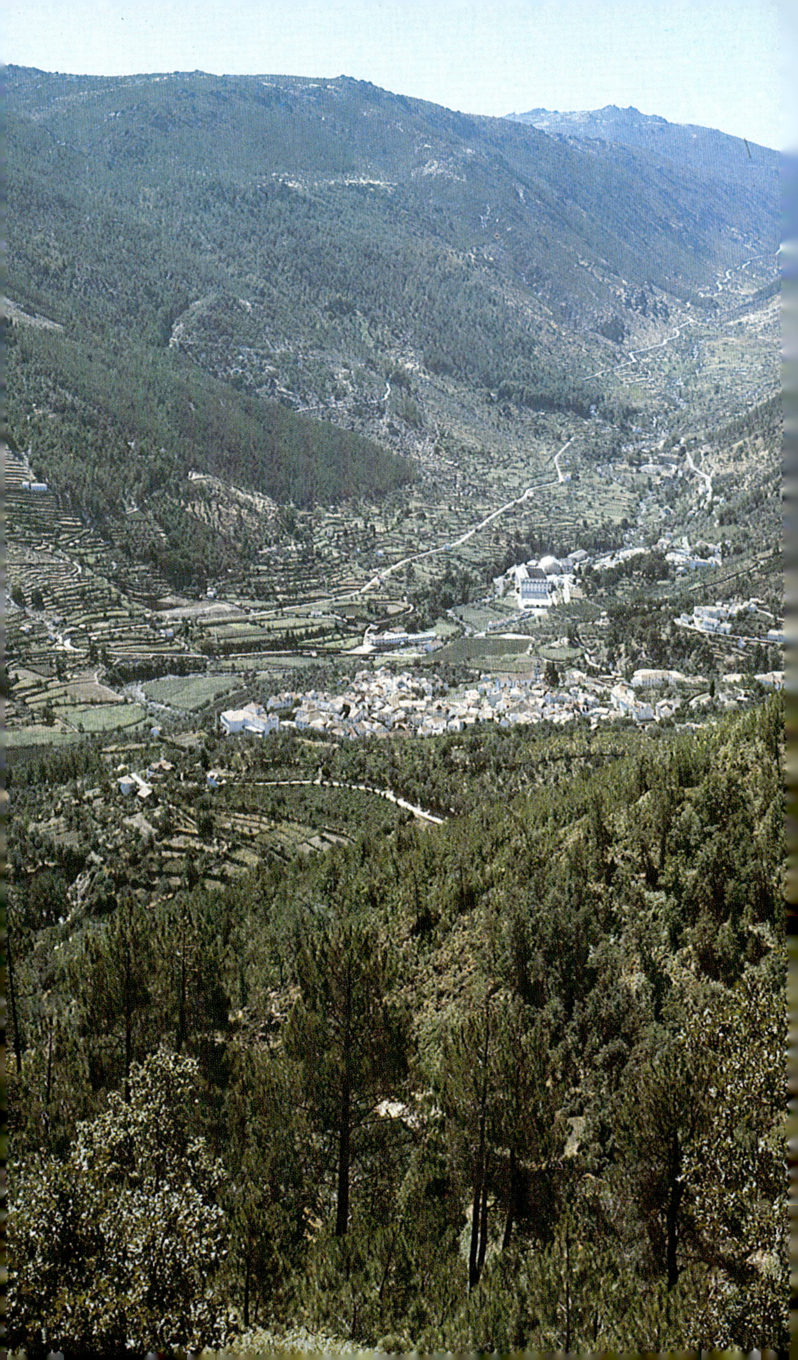

The cathedral, originally a 13th c. Romanesque building, is today a mixture of Gothic, Renaissance and Manueline architecture. The Manueline vaulted roof, the cloisters with their lovely azulejo decoration and a museum in the chapter house, rich in art treasures, all contribute to making the cathedral one of the most important in Portugal.

Apart from a four-star hotel, Viseu also has more modest accommodation to offer.

- Parque Fontelo and Hotel Grão Vasco.
- Parque Fontelo.
- Hotel Grão Vasco.
- O Cortiço.

Guarda Alt. 1050 m; Pop. 15,000

Situated in the foothills of the Serra da Estrela, Guarda is the highest town in Portugal. Its focal point is the cathedral which has elements of the Gothic, Manueline and Renaissance styles of architecture. Inside, the altar-piece, attributed to Jean de Rouen, has a large number of figures and is of particular interest.

A special tip

Although difficult to reach, the *Caramulo Museum of Modern Art* is situated in the midst of the 1,000-m-high Serra do Caramulo. This museum houses works by famous artists including Picasso, Chagall, Dali, Dufy and Léger. There is also a motor museum with a varied collection of old cars, motor-cycles and even bicycles.

Lamego Alt. 500 m; Pop. 10,000

The little town of Lamego nestles among the mountainous scenery of the Serra do Marão. It was here in 1143 that Afonso Henriques was recognised as the first king of Portugal. The most interesting place to visit is, undoubtedly, the 18th c. shrine of *Nossa Senhora dos Remédios*, which was built in the middle of a large park on top of a hill. You have to climb 600 steps to reach this Baroque church which has the same feeling about it as the Bom Jesus in Braga. Good views over the Douro valley can be enjoyed from the top and also from the terraces which break the monotony of the long flight of steps. On another hill overlooking the old town can be seen the ruins of a 12th c. castle.

The other very interesting place is the *Museu Regional* situated in the main square in a former 18th c. palace. Paintings by Vasco Fernandes and a collection of 16th c. tapestries are among the most valuable treasures of this large museum.

- To *Taronca*, 14 km away, where there is the monastery church of *São João de Taronca*.

Funchal market

The Island provinces in the Atlantic

A small part of the Far East and an association with Brazil are all that remain today of the wealthy Portuguese Empire which was once world-wide. The island groups of Madeira and the Azores, which were discovered by the Portuguese in the first half of the 15th c., are now integrated into the Portuguese system of government as provinces even though they are, in fact, independent.

Because of the favourable climate and beautiful scenery the islands, Madeira in particular, have over the years developed into Portugal's show-piece for holidaymakers.

Madeira — an Atlantic Paradise

The island group of Madeira, situated approximately 1,000 km from the mainland to the south-west of Lisbon and in the same latitude as Beirut, consists of the main island of Madeira, the little island of *Porto Santo* (pop. 3,000) 35 km to the north-east, and three uninhabited islands. 300,000 people live on the island of Madeira which is 57 km long and 22 km wide. The mild Atlantic climate is the most equable in the whole of Europe. The highest daytime temperatures are, on average, 25° in summer and 18° in winter. The average sea temperatures from June to November vary between 20° and 23°, while in December they remain close to 19° and never drop below 17°. Although it rains very little in summer there is more precipitation in winter. For the holidaymaker Madeira is one of the few places which can remind you of paradise. There are no wild animals and for centuries there have been no natural disasters. In fact nature has hardly been disturbed at all. The pace of life is relaxed, the people friendly and spring is never-ending.

When people talk about Madeira they are usually referring to Funchal, but Funchal, of course, is far from being Madeira. Cruise ships dock here, charter jets land and over 90% of holidaymakers stay in Funchal. It is home to one-third of the population of the islands and the few buildings which are of historical or cultural value are to be found here. It is an important business and commercial centre and possesses many sporting

Madeira — terraced fields

and recreational facilities.

Beyond the capital, however, the true characteristics of the island become apparent. Its solitude, the mountains rising to 1,861 m, the ravines, and the coastline with huge Atlantic breakers crashing on to the cliffs all contribute to the rugged beauty of the islands. The south coast is the more fertile part of Madeira, with its blossom-covered terraces, orchards, vineyards and extensive banana plantations.

On the more sparsely populated north coast formidable cliffs enclose small fishing villages and friendly little towns, some of which nestle deep inside the narrow romantic valleys. The Atlantic breakers are particularly rough on the west coast of the island, while there is a promontory on the east coast which is gradually disappearing into the sea off *Ponta de S. Lourenço*.

The interior of the island is quite mountainous and is rich in woodland and wild flowers, even at the highest altitudes. Three mountains rise to a height of over 1,800 m and several others to over 1,600 m.

Funchal's new holiday image

For many years Funchal was favoured mostly by the British. It served as a holiday or retirement spot and was particularly popular in winter months, especially at the New Year when its world-famous firework display was held. This, however, does not apply any more and it is not only older people convalescing who come here and who can be seen in the parks, bars and hotel swimming pools, but also much younger people of many nationalities.

Funchal lies on a hillside thickly carpeted with flowers and trees. Houses interspersed with gardens, vineyards and banana plantations mingle on the slopes as far as *Monte*, the upper part of the town situated at 550 m. It is from here that Madeira's most famous tourist attraction begins — the journey in traditional toboggans down the steep little alleyways to the town below. The Manueline cathedral which has a remarkable wooden ceiling and a Chapel of the Holy Sacrament, the Natural History Museum with an aquarium, and the sub-tropical *São Francisco* gardens on the Avenida Arriaga are all well worth seeing. The new Municipal Park on the Praça do Infante has some beautiful flowerbeds and flowering trees. In the upper part of the town is the *Nazaré* Chapel, decorated with beautiful tiles, from where a splendid view can be obtained. Do not waste time looking for bathing beaches on Madeira; all first-class

Typical Madeiran cottage

hotels have large swimming pools and some even have well constructed pathways from the cliffs to the sea, where the water, even near the harbour, is noticeably clear.

Madeira is well off for sporting and recreational facilities.

Casa de Turista for lace, pottery, embroidery etc.

Frequent performances in hotels and resorts. Fado bars.

The Azores

For those of you who take an interest in weather reports, the name 'Azores' is synonymous with fine weather. Situated 1,500 km from Lisbon and 4,000 km from New York, the archipelago covers an area between 30° and 39° north in latitude and between 25° and 31° west in longitude.

The group of islands discovered in 1431 by Gonçalo Velho Cabral has a population today of approximately 300,000, and covers an area of 2,344 sq. km. The mild equable climate with an annual average temperature of 17° means that three harvests a year are possible. The main crops are pineapples, grapes, tea and sugar cane. Cattle are raised, while fishing and the canning industry both play an important role in the economy. As yet tourist accommodation is limited.

São Miguel

'The Green Island', so called because of its sub-tropical vegetation, has about 172,000 inhabitants and, with an area of 747 sq. km, is the largest in the Azores. The mountainous east and west sides of the island still show evidence of the volcanic origins of the archipelago. The craters, however, though emitting steam, are no longer dangerous.

The capital, *Ponta Delgada*, with a population of 35,000, is a picturesque little harbour town with several 16th c. buildings which are worth seeing. There are two good class hotels and a number of small hotels and guest houses, all of which offer excellent value for money.

The most popular and famous place which tourists visit in São Miguel and, indeed, in the whole of the Azores, is *Vale das Furnas*. Twenty-three thermal springs have given the town its reputation of being one of the world's best spas. The Hotel *Terra Nostra* has not only a thermal swimming pool but also a magnificent park.

Do take a trip to the *Caldeira das Sete Cidades* crater. It is at the bottom of a volcano with a diameter of 5 km and has two lakes, one of which is green and the other blue.

Santa Maria Pop. 13,500

77 km from São Miguel, it is the most easterly island in the Azores and covers an area of 97 sq. km. The main town of *Vila do Porto* is famous for its traditional age-old pottery. A very picturesque scene is created by the teams of oxen used for drawing carts. Close to *São Lourenço* there is a very good sandy beach, perfect for bathing.

Terceira Pop. 78,000

This was the third island in the Azores to be discovered and populated. *Angra do Heroísmo*, with 15,000 inhabitants, the capital of the island and home of its cathedral, is a lovely harbour town, set in a bay, with two 15th c. monasteries.

Graciosa Pop. 7,200

The second smallest island in the Azores, Graciosa is famous for its excellent wines and for its sulphur springs, *Furna do Enxofre*. The main town is Santa Cruz with 2,000 inhabitants.

São Jorge Pop. 13,000

São Jorge is well known for its tasty cheeses. The inhabitants make a living from farming and cattle raising. The main town is Velas with a population of 2,000.

Pico Pop. 18,000

The island of Pico has Portugal's highest mountain. From the summit (2,351 m) on a clear day you can get a good view over the whole of the archipelago. The main town is Lajes, with a population of 2,300.

Faial Pop. 21,000

The inhabitants live mainly off the land but it is interesting as a holiday centre. *Horta*, the principal town with a population of 7,000, has a good harbour and a small beach with an old fort. In 1957 a new volcano, *Vulcão dos Capelinhos*, erupted near Faial forming a new island.

Flores

The masses of hydrangeas which cover Flores make it one of the most beautiful islands in the Azores. Extinct volcanoes, crater lakes, waterfalls and quaint little villages all add to its charm.

Corvo

Corvo is only 17 sq. km in size and has 470 inhabitants. Straight paved streets, and houses whose doors are never closed — that is Corvo, a paradise in the watery wastes of the Atlantic.

Useful things to know...

Before you go

Climate

The height and extent of the mountains and their position relative to the coast play a considerable part in determining the climatic differences between the various parts of Portugal. As in this country, from June until August are the favourite months with holidaymakers, but the seaside resorts near Lisbon and in the Algarve are busy right up to October. The winter holiday traffic in the coastal resorts, with their favourable climate, is now increasing every year.

A temperature chart is given below which should help you choose the best time to take your holiday.

Average climate over the last 10 years
AT = mean monthly air temperature (day/night)
WT = mean monthly water temperature

Month	Algarve (Faro) AT	WT	Lisbon AT	WT	Oporto AT	WT
January	15.3/ 9.0	15	13.9/ 7.8	14	13.2/ 4.7	14
February	16.1/ 9.5	15	15.2/ 8.1	14	14.2/ 5.0	13
March	17.5/11.1	15	17.3/10.0	14	16.3/ 7.5	13
April	19.7/12.5	16	19.6/11.5	15	18.4/ 8.8	14
May	21.9/14.4	17	21.4/12.9	16	19.6/10.8	15
June	25.2/17.5	18	24.8/15.4	17	22.6/13.4	16
July	28.2/19.5	19	27.4/17.0	18	24.7/14.6	17
August	28.2/19.9	20	27.7/17.3	19	25.0/14.6	18
September	25.7/18.6	20	25.9/16.5	19	23.7/13.6	18
October	22.4/15.7	19	22.3/14.2	18	20.8/10.8	17
November	18.9/12.6	17	17.2/11.0	16	16.7/ 7.8	15
December	16.2/ 9.8	16	14.5/ 8.5	15	13.7/ 5.4	15

Lace making

Holiday Accommodation

There are a large number of luxury hotels in Portugal. The charge for full board per person varies from £50 to £100 per day. Facilities and services in these hotels not only compare favourably with those in other countries, but sometimes even surpass them. In a good middle-class hotel the cost of full board for a room with a shower or bath lies somewhere between £30 and £55 a day. In addition, especially in the coastal resorts, there are a large number of *pensões* (pensions), the majority of which also have a small restaurant. On the Algarve, in and around Lisbon and on the island of Madeira apartment houses and bungalows suitable for self-catering holidays have sprung up, and there are numerous camping sites, a full list of which can be obtained from the Portuguese Tourist Office.

The state owned *pousadas*, a cheaper form of guest house, are run by the Portuguese Tourist Office and are peculiar to Portugal. They are usually sited in quite attractive places and are furnished in traditional local style. These guest houses also serve as small restaurants, specialising in regional dishes. They seldom have more than 30 rooms and the prices, considering what is provided, are extraordinarily low. To date there are 30 such pousadas throughout the country. Just as typical, regional and small in size, are the guest houses known as *estalagem*. In contrast to the pousadas, however, they are privately run and usually more expensive.

Insurance

It is advisable to take out additional health insurance for the duration of the holiday in order that treatment as a private patient can be obtained.

Getting to Portugal

By air: This is the most popular form of transport. Lisbon is served from Great Britain by British Airways and TAP (Air Portugal), although there are also many charter companies offering flights at very reasonable prices. The principal airports are at Lisbon, Oporto and Faro. Flight connections to Terceira and São Miguel in the Azores leave from Lisbon 4–5 times a week.

By rail: The journey from London to Lisbon via Paris and Irun/Hendaye takes just over 36 hours. Sleepers and couchettes are available and there is a motorail service through France.

By road: More and more people are travelling to Portugal by car using the cross-channel ferry services. The shortest distance between London and Lisbon is 1,564 km.

By sea: There are no regular services from Great Britain but Brittany Ferries operate a service from Plymouth to Santander (Spain) from where there are onward connections by rail.

Immigration and Customs Regulations

Citizens of the EEC countries who do not intend to stay in Portugal for more than two months require a valid identity card or passport. If a longer stay is desired, then permission must be sought and full details obtained from a Portuguese Consulate.

Unlimited amounts of foreign money may be imported into Portugal but it must be declared to Customs if the equivalent value is more than 100,000 Escudos (about £400). Portuguese currency, however, may be imported without restriction. The export of foreign exchange is, if the equivalent value exceeds 25,000 Esc. (£100), only permitted within the limits of the amount declared on entry. The maximum amount allowed for the export of Escudos is 50,000 (£200).

Customs: As a member of the EEC Portugal has the same duty-free allowances as the other countries of the community. These are: 300 cigarettes or 75 cigars or 400 gr. tobacco; 1.5 litres of spirits (over 22% alcohol) or 3 litres of sparkling or fortified wine and 4 litres of other wine; 75 gr. perfume and .375 litres of toilet water. If any of the above have been bought in a duty-free shop or on a ship or aircraft the allowances are approximately one third less.

If you are travelling by car, you must have with you your driving licence, your log book and green card. It is also compulsory in Portugal to have third-party insurance cover. It is suggested that you take out short-term comprehensive cover; in the event of an accident, you should inform your insurance company and Consulate immediately.

During your stay
Currency and Prices

The Portuguese monetary unit is the Escudo, which consists of 100 centavos. 100 Escudos are the equivalent of about 37 pence and conversely £1 = 260 Esc. As the Escudo rate varies from day to day, it is always best to enquire from a bank. Escudo is abbreviated in Portugal by the $ sign. Don't be alarmed by prices which seem ridiculous, though, and remember that they are being quoted in Escudos, not in dollars! The dollar sign comes between Escudos and Centavos. The current coins in circulation are for 1, 2½, 5 and 10 Escudos, and 10, 20 and 50 Centavos, while there are notes for 20, 50, 100, 500 and 1,000 Escudos.

Electricity

The standard current in most places in Portugal is 220 volts and in the Azores 110 volts A.C. Sockets are of the usual Continental pattern.

Opening times

The banks are open on Monday to Friday from 8.30 to 11.45 a.m. and from 1 to 2.45 p.m.

Most shops are open on weekdays from 9 a.m. to 1 p.m. and from 3 to 7 p.m. On Saturdays they close at 1 p.m. but in tourist areas some shops remain open until late in the evening.

Post

Post Offices are normally open all day from 9 a.m. to 6 p.m. The main Post Offices in Lisbon and Oporto are open 24 hours a day.

It is possible to buy stamps, if you are lucky, at a tobacconist's but otherwise you will have to go to a Post Office. Postal rates to England are: postcards 45 Esc., letters 52 Esc., express delivery 90 Esc.

Religious services

In most places there are only Catholic church services held at the usual times. In the large tourist resorts some services are held in English, while in Lisbon there are churches of many other denominations, including a Synagogue in the Rua Alexandre Herculano where services are held at 8 a.m. and 8 p.m. daily and on Saturdays at 9 a.m. and 7 p.m.

Telephone and radio

Only the larger towns have public telephone kiosks. If you wish to make a telephone call, the best plan is to phone from your hotel or from a Post Office.

The news in English is broadcast by Radio Algarve in the morning and early evening.

Tipping

In hotels and restaurants a 15% service charge is included in the price but an additional nominal tip will, of course, always be appreciated and the Portuguese themselves are usually willing to give something in return for good service. For taxis, cloakroom attendants, porters etc. it is usual to tip between 5 and 10 Escudos.

Transport in Portugal
Air services

The Portuguese internal airlines network, served by TAP, links the airports of Lisbon, Oporto and Faro on the mainland, as well as providing flights from Lisbon to Funchal on the Island of Madeira and to the Azores. The return fare for flights Lisbon-Faro or Lisbon-Oporto is 9,752 Escudos (approximately £37.50). In addition, there are smaller airports in 22 towns, including Braga and Bragança, all of which are served by LAR (Ligações Aereos Regionais). Bookings may be made at any TAP (Air Portugal) office.

Local buses/trams and taxis

Buses operate in most towns, even in the smaller ones, and some of the larger cities have trams. Fares on both forms of transport are inexpensive and taxis are also cheap, but you should be careful to see that the meter in the taxi is working properly. It is, however, advisable to agree on a price with the taxi-driver before undertaking any long journey.

Car hire

Cars may be hired in all the larger towns. The basic charge for a Renault 5, for example, would be a little more than £10 per day, in addition to which there may be a mileage charge of about 10p per km. Cheaper rates can often be found, particularly some without the mileage charge. It is important to find out whether or not the hire car is fully insured. Since July 1987 21 filling stations selling lead-free petrol have come into operation.

Railways/long-distance buses

Portugal has a good railway network, but apart from international expresses, trains seem to be somewhat on the slow side. Fares are, however, cheaper than in the UK. A wide network of bus routes extends to even the smallest towns.

Important addresses

Diplomatic and Consular Offices

British Embassy
Rua São Domingos à Lapa 35–37,
Lisbon; tel. (01) 66 11 91.

British Consulate
Avenida da Boavista 3072,
Oporto; tel. via operator.

Airlines

TAP — Air Portugal
3 Praça Marquês de Pombal,
Lisbon; tel. (01) 53 88 52.

British Airways
Avenida da Liberdade 23–27,
Lisbon; tel. (01) 36 09 31.

Rua de Júlio Dinis 778/11,
Oporto; tel. (02) 69 45 75.

Tourist Information Offices

For all Portugal
Palácio Foz, Praça dos Restauradores,
Lisbon; tel. (01) 36 33 14.

For Lisbon
Rua Jardim de Regedor,
Lisbon; tel. (01) 32 55 27.

In Great Britain
New Bond Street House,
1–5 New Bond Street,
London W1Y 0DB; tel. (01) 493 3873.

Useful words and phrases

Being able to use a few words of Portuguese can be very useful. The Portuguese people greatly appreciate any attempt to use their language, however faulty the pronunciation.

In Portuguese the stress on words ending in a, e, o, m or s (the great majority) is on the last syllable but one; words with any other ending have the stress on the last syllable. The exceptions to these two rules have an accent on the stressed syllable.

O or a at the end of a word is sounded like an unstressed e. A tilde (~) over a vowel causes the sound to be nasalised; em and am at the end of a word sound like a nasal 'aing' (Belém = Belaing). Lh and nh have the sounds of ly and ny (senhor = senyor). S is like an English s before vowels but like z between vowels and like sh before hard consonants or at the end of a word. C is like k before a, o and u and like s before e and i; ç = s; ch = sh. G is hard (as in 'go') before a, o and u and like the s in 'measure' before e and i.

please	faz favor
thank you (very much)	(muito) obrigado
yes/no	sim/não
excuse me	desculpe
do you speak English?	O senhor fala inglês?
I do not understand	não compreendo
good morning	bom dia
good afternoon	boa tarde
good night	boa noite
good bye	adeus/até àvista
how much?	quanto custa?
I should like	queria
a room with private bath	um quarto com banho
the bill, please	faz favor a conta
everything included	tudo incluido
when is it open / shut?	a que horas está aberto / fechado
where is ... street? the road to...?	onde é rua ...? a estrade para...?
how far?	que distância?
left	à esquerda
right	à direita
straight on	a direito
Post Office	Correio
Railway station	Estação
Town Hall	Paços de Concelho
Exchange Office	Câmbio
Police Station	Posto de Policia
Public telephone	Posto telefonico
Tourist Information Office	Posto de Turismo
Doctor	Médico
Chemist	Farmácia
toilet	lavabos
ladies	senhoras
gentlemen	senhores
engaged	ocupado
free	livre
entrance	entrada
exit	saída
today / tomorrow	hoje / amanhã
Sunday / Monday	domingo / segunda-feira
Tuesday / Wednesday	terça-feira / quarta-feira
Thursday / Friday	quinta-feira / sexta-feira
Saturday / holiday	sábado / dia de festa
0 zero	
1 um, uma	
2 dois, duas	
3 três	
4 quatro	
5 cinco	
6 seis	
7 sete	
8 oito	
9 nove	
10 dez	
11 onze	
12 doze	
20 vinte	
50 cinquenta	
100 cem, cento	